# Contents

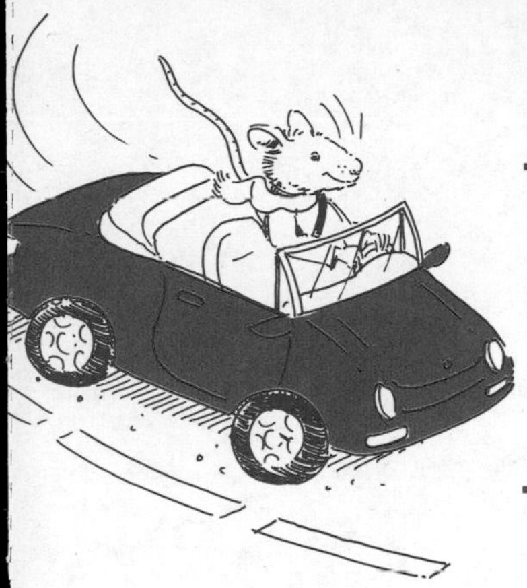


Back to School . . . . . . . . . . . . . . . . . . . . B-1

Theme 1 All Together Now
Week 1 . . . . . . . . . . . . . . . . . . . . . . . . 1
Week 2 . . . . . . . . . . . . . . . . . . . . . . . . 18
Week 3 . . . . . . . . . . . . . . . . . . . . . . . . 35

Theme 2 Surprise!
Week 1 . . . . . . . . . . . . . . . . . . . . . . . . 53
Week 2 . . . . . . . . . . . . . . . . . . . . . . . . 71
Week 3 . . . . . . . . . . . . . . . . . . . . . . . . 86

Theme 3 Let's Look Around!
Week 1 . . . . . . . . . . . . . . . . . . . . . . . . 101
Week 2 . . . . . . . . . . . . . . . . . . . . . . . . 117
Week 3 . . . . . . . . . . . . . . . . . . . . . . . . 131
Spelling Review . . . . . . . . . . . . . . . . . . . 145

Theme 4 Family and Friends
Week 1 . . . . . . . . . . . . . . . . . . . . . . . . 147
Week 2 . . . . . . . . . . . . . . . . . . . . . . . . 161
Week 3 . . . . . . . . . . . . . . . . . . . . . . . . 176
Spelling Review . . . . . . . . . . . . . . . . . . . 189


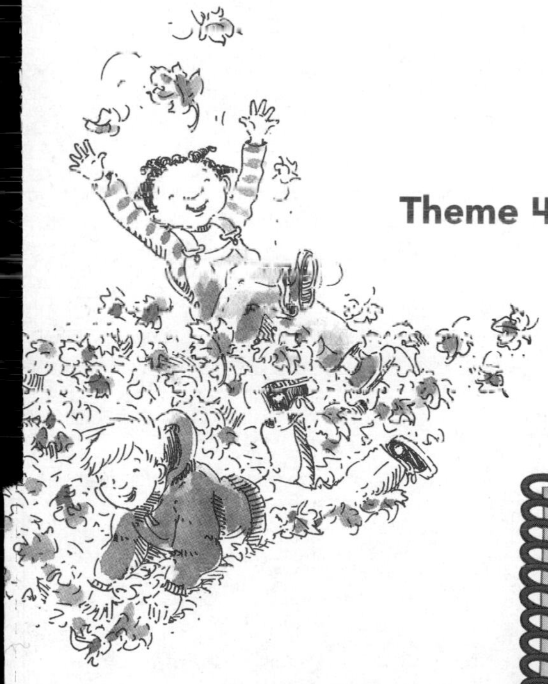


My Handbook . . . . . . . . . . . . . . . . . . . . . 191
Alphafriends . . . . . . . . . . . . . . . . . . . . 194
Phonics/Decoding Strategy . . . . . . 196
Reading Strategies . . . . . . . . . . . . 197
Writing the Alphabet . . . . . . . . . . . 198
Spelling . . . . . . . . . . . . . . . . . . . . . . 206
How to Study a Word
Special Words for Writing
Take-Home Word Lists

Punchouts


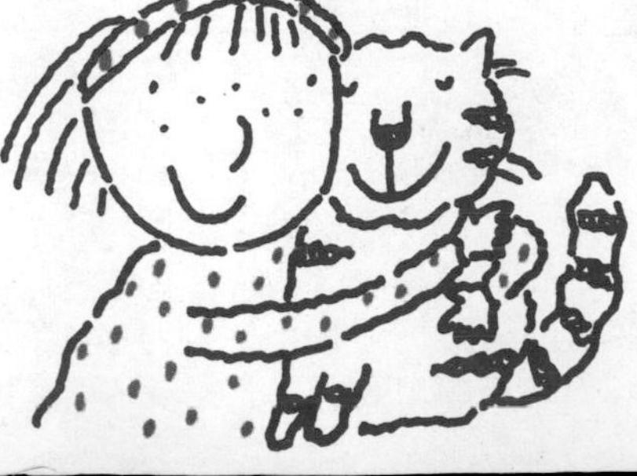

Back to School

Summarize Strategy
*My Best Friend*

Name ______________________

# What Happened?

**The picture shows what happens at the beginning of *My Best Friend*. Draw a picture of something that happens in the middle of the story. Then draw what happens at the end.**

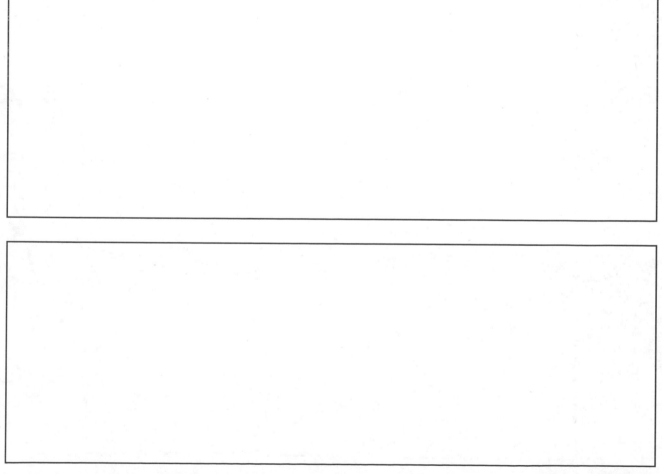

Name ______________________________

# My Own Best Friend

**Draw a picture of you and your best friend doing something you love to do together.**

Name ______________________________

# Alphabet Review

Andy Apple

Benny Bear

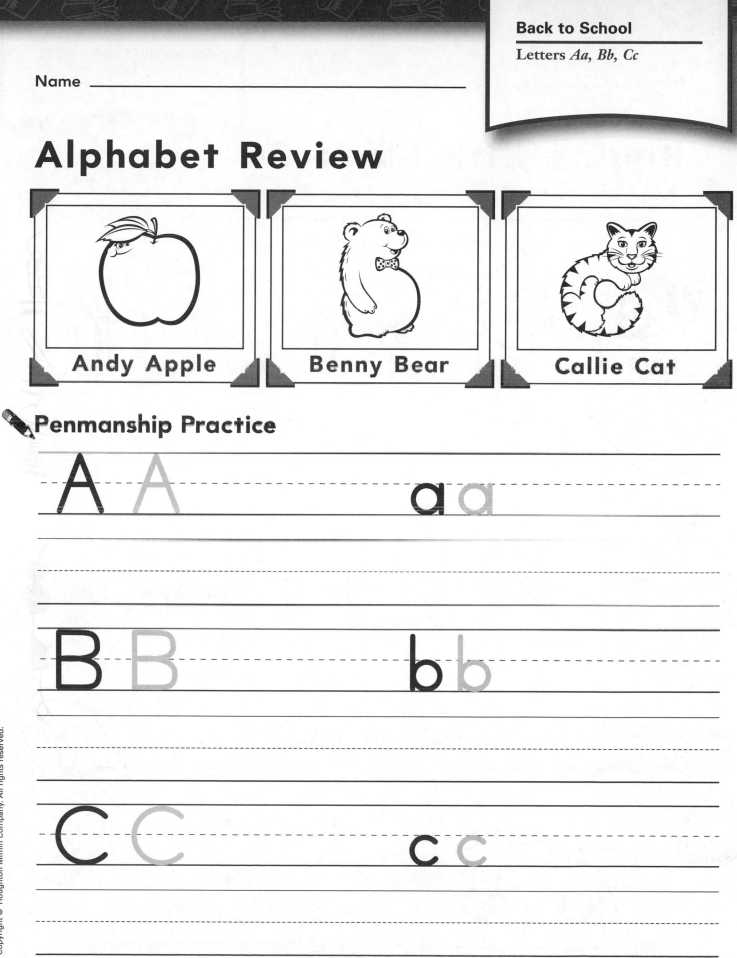

Callie Cat

## Penmanship Practice

A A a a

B B b b

C C c c

Name ______________________________

# Begins with Bb or Cc

**Phonics** Circle each picture whose name begins like the Alphafriend's name.

Bb

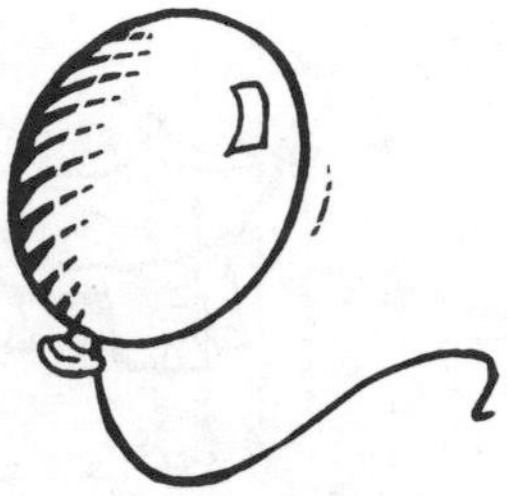

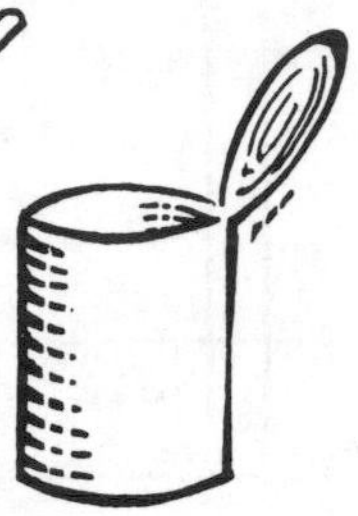

Cc

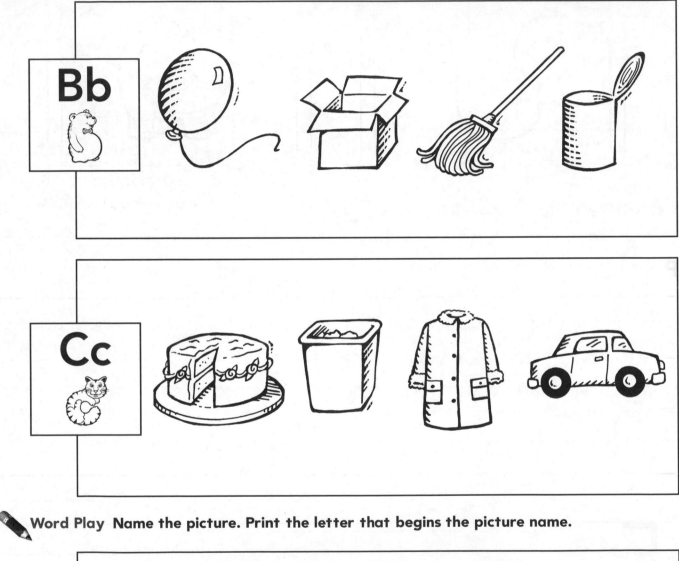

**Word Play** Name the picture. Print the letter that begins the picture name.

a b c

Name ______________________

# Alphabet Review

Dudley Duck

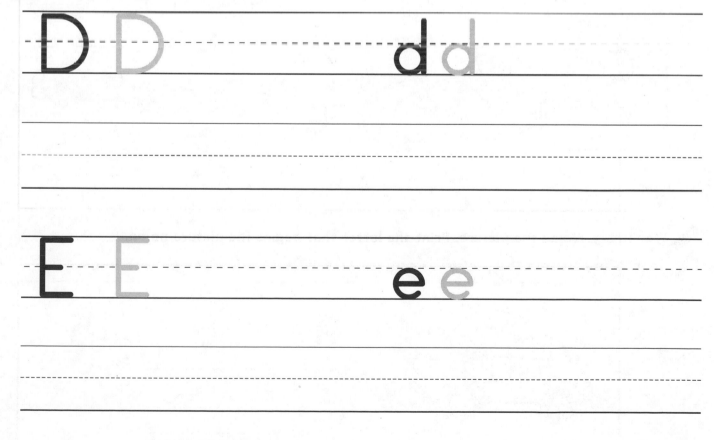

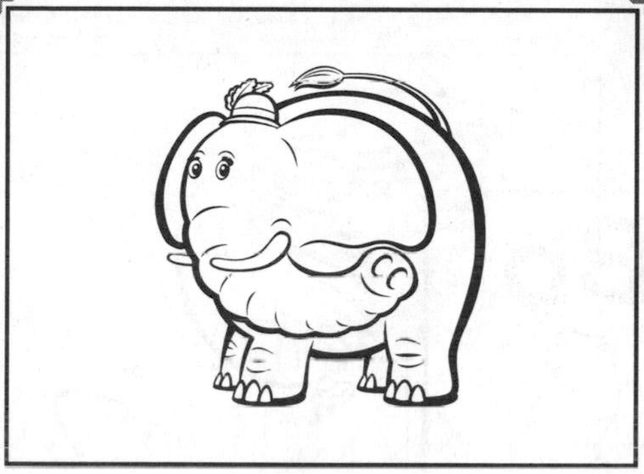

Edna Elephant

## Penmanship Practice

D D d d

E E e e

Name ______________________________

# The Letters Dd and Ee

**Phonics** Draw a line from the Dd to pictures whose names begin with that letter sound.

Dd

**Draw a line from the E to the matching letters.**

E e E e E

e

E e E E

e

E e E

**Word Play** Name the picture. Print the letter that begins the picture name.

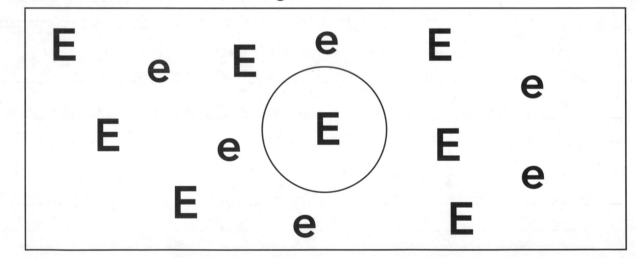

a d b

Name ____________________

# Alphabet Review

Fifi Fish

Gertie Goose

Hattie Horse

## Penmanship Practice

F F f f

G G g g

H H h h

Name ______________________________

Back to School

Sounds and Letters *Ff, Gg, Hh*

# Begins with Ff, Gg, or Hh

**Phonics** **Circle each picture whose name begins like the Alphafriend's name.**

Ff

Gg

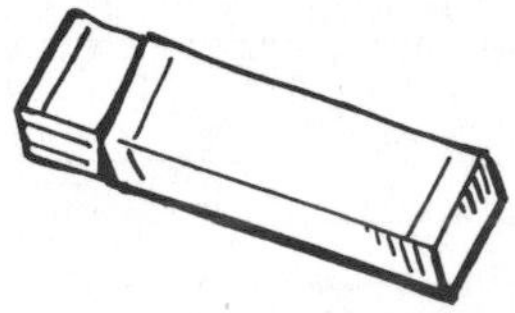

Hh

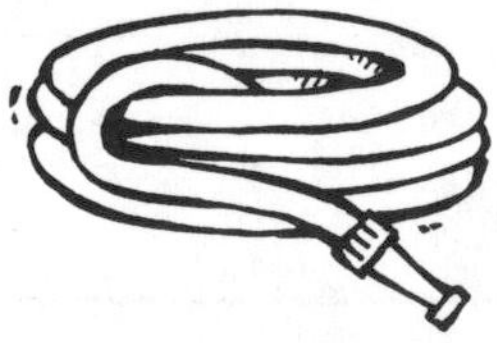

**Word Play** **Name the picture. Print the letter that begins the picture name.**

d e f

______________

Name ____________________

# Alphabet Review

Iggy Iguana

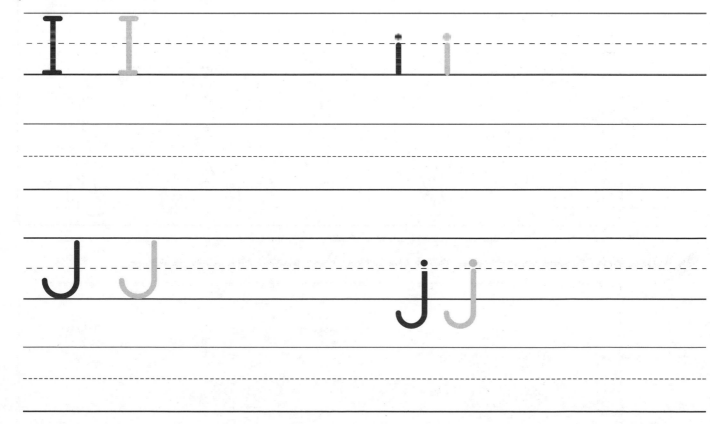

Jumping Jill

## Penmanship Practice

I I i i

J J j j

Name ________________________________

# The Letters Ii and Jj

**Phonics** Draw a line from the i to the matching letters.

i I i I
I I i I
i i I i i

Draw a line from the Jj to the pictures whose names begin with that letter sound.

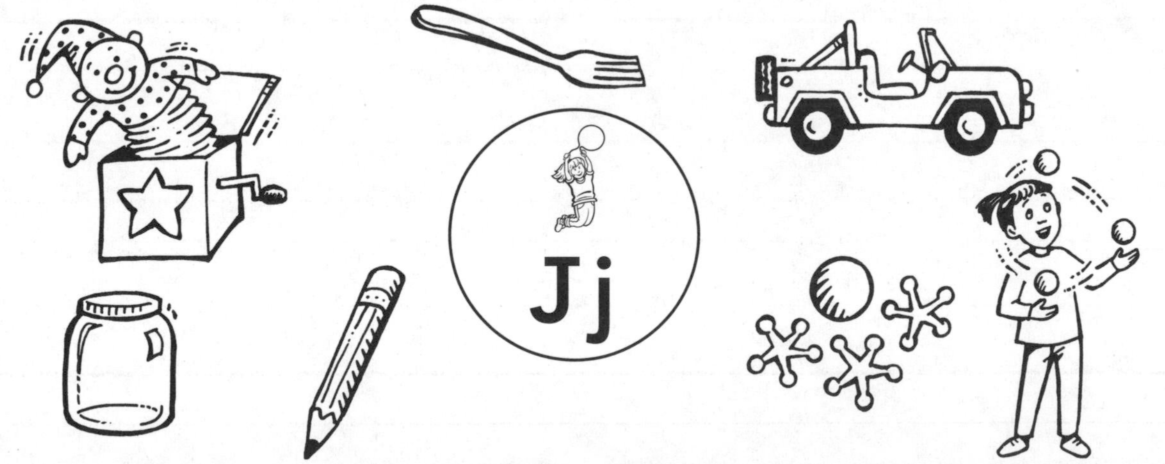


**Word Play** Name the picture. Print the letter that begins the picture name.

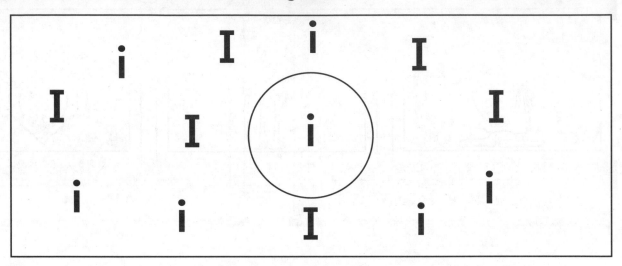

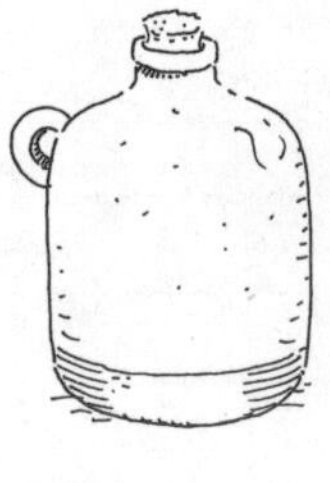

e j m

______________

Name ______________________________

# Alphabet Review

Keely Kangaroo

Larry Lion

Mimi Mouse

## Penmanship Practice

K K k k

L L l l

M M m m

Back to School

Sounds and Letters *Kk, Ll, Mm*

Name ______________________________

# Begins with Kk, Ll, or Mm

**Phonics** Circle each picture whose name begins like the Alphafriend's name.

**Kk**

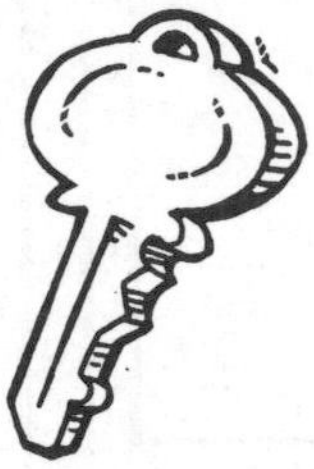

**Ll**

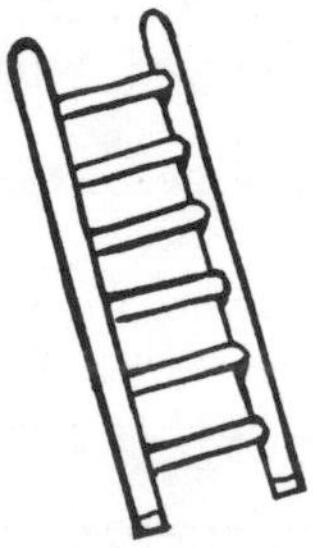

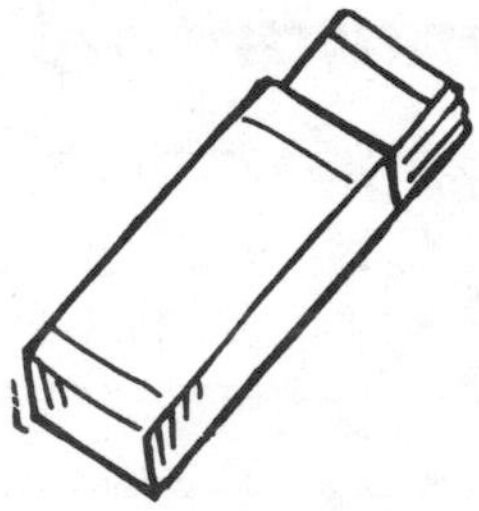

**Mm**

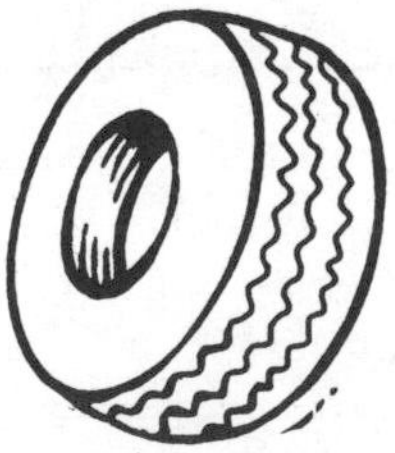

**Word Play** Name the picture. Print the letter that begins the picture name.

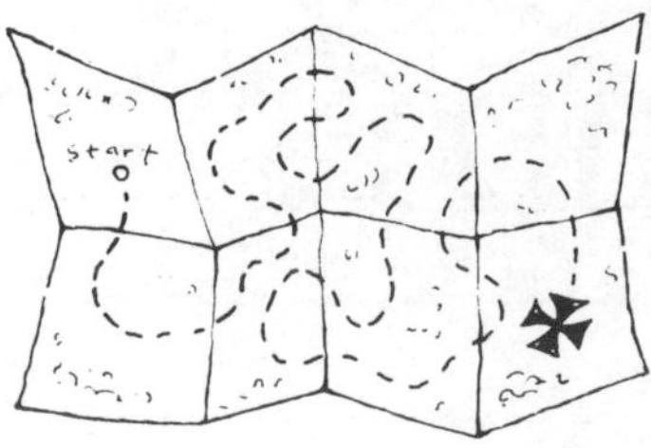


l d m

______

Name ______________________________

# Alphabet Review

Nyle Noodle

Ozzie Octopus

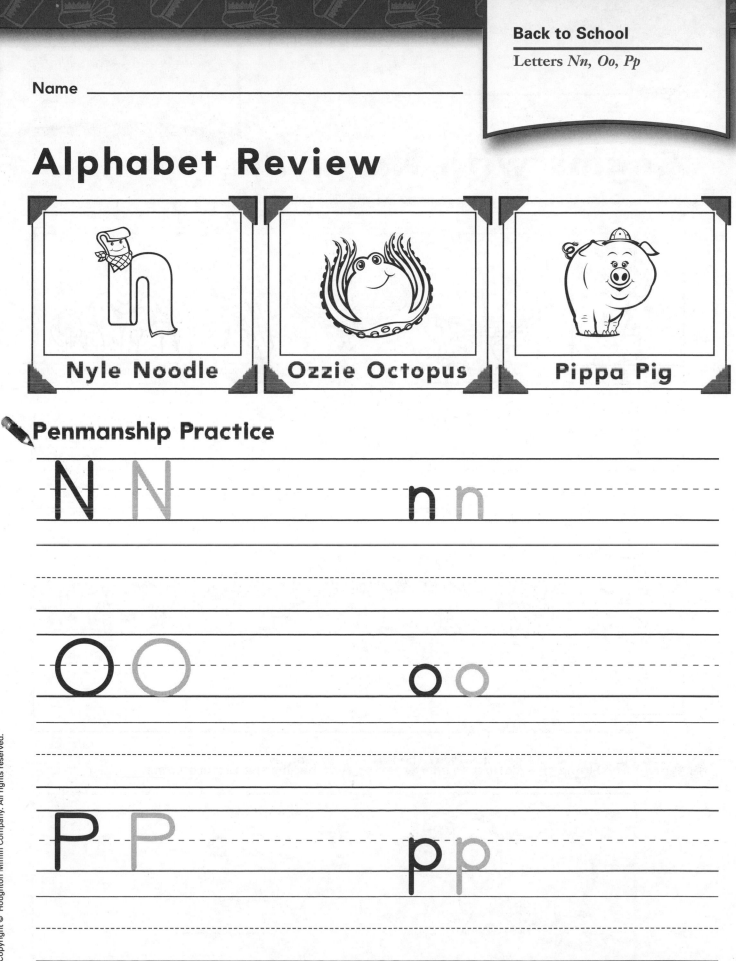

Pippa Pig

## Penmanship Practice

N N n n

O O o o

P P p p

Name ______________________________

# Begins with Nn or Pp

**Phonics** Circle each picture whose name begins like the Alphafriend's name.

**Nn**

**Pp**

**Word Play** Name the picture. Print the letter that begins the picture name.

g e p

______

Name ______________________________

# Alphabet Review

## Penmanship Practice

Q Q q q

R R r r

S S s s

Back to School

Sounds and Letters *Qq, Rr, Ss*

Name ______________________________

# Begins with Qq, Rr, or Ss

**Phonics** Circle each picture whose name begins like the Alphafriend's name.

**Qq**

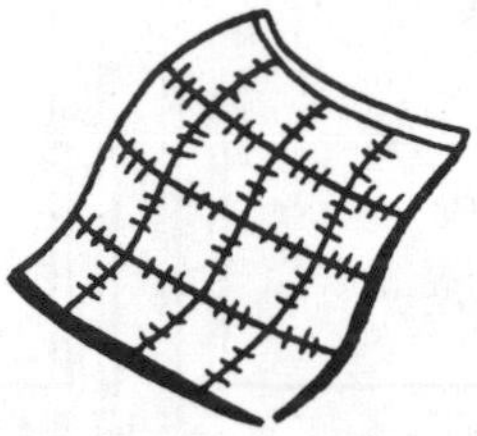

**Rr**

**Ss**

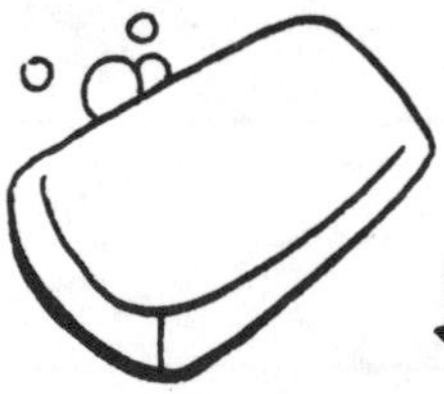

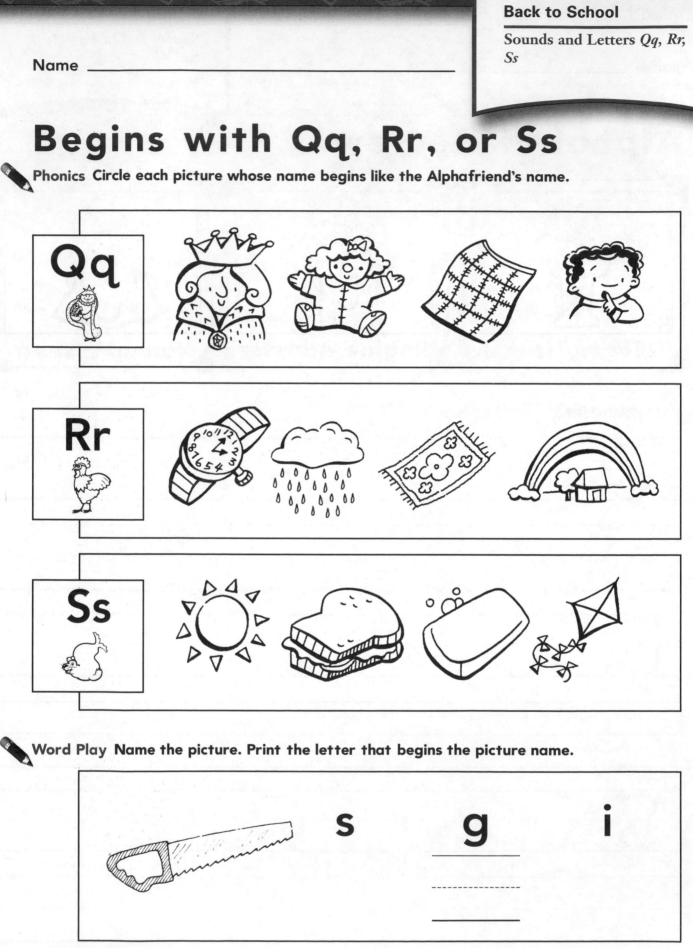

**Word Play** Name the picture. Print the letter that begins the picture name.

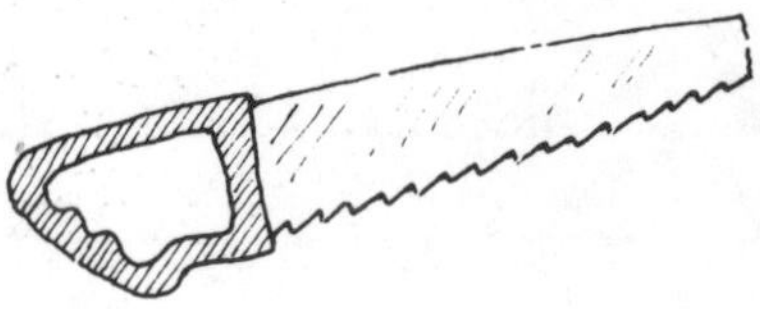

s g i

Name ____________________

# Alphabet Review

Tiggy Tiger

Umbie Umbrella

Vinny Volcano

## Penmanship Practice

T T t t

U U u u

V V v v

Name ______________________________

# Begins with Tt or Vv

**Phonics** **Circle each picture whose name begins like the Alphafriend's name.**

**Tt**

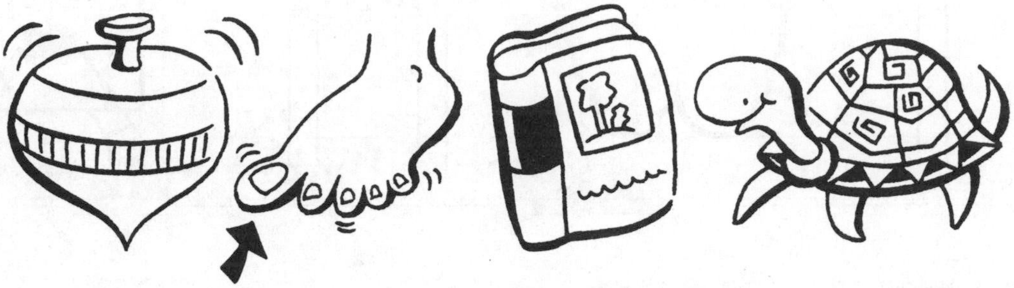

**Vv**

**Word Play** **Name the picture. Print the letter that begins the picture name.**

u t h

______

Name ______________________________

# Alphabet Review

Willy Worm

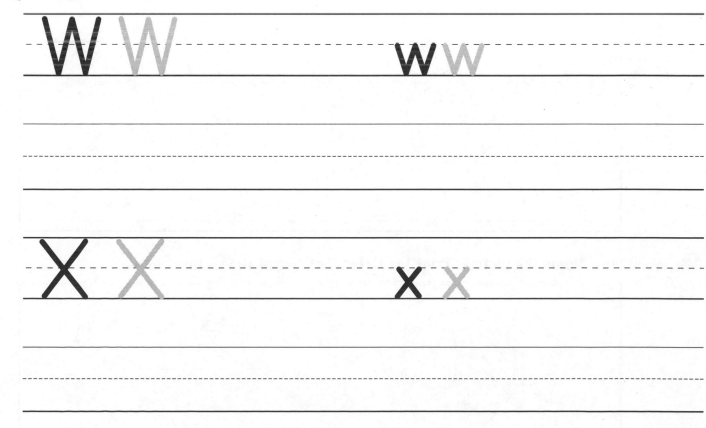

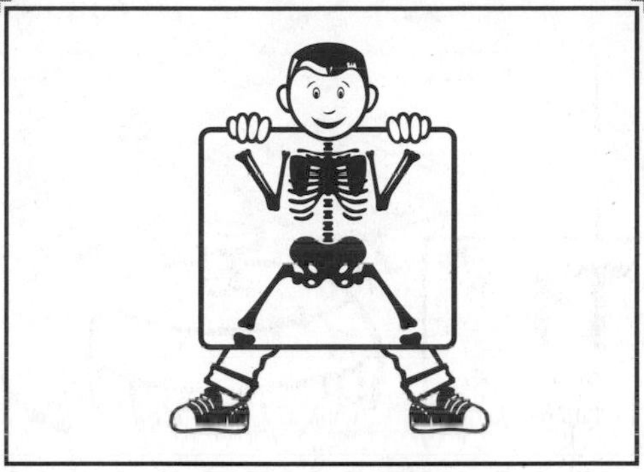

Mr. X-Ray

## Penmanship Practice

W W w w

X X x x

Name ______________________________

# The Sounds for Ww and Xx

**Phonics** **Draw a line from the Ww to the pictures whose names begin with that letter sound.**

**Draw a line from the Xx to the pictures whose names have the /ks/ sound.**

**Word Play** **Name the picture. Print the letter that begins the picture name.**

f   w   o

______________

Name ______________________________

# Alphabet Review

Yetta Yo-Yo

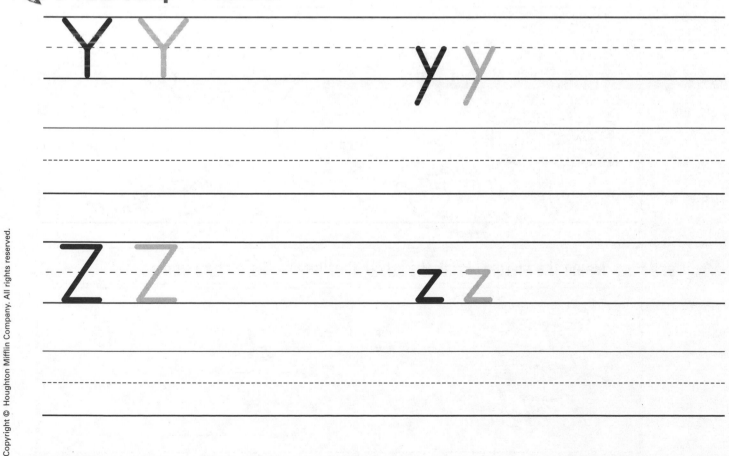

Zelda Zebra

## Penmanship Practice

Y Y          y y

Z Z          z z

Name ______________________________

# Begins with Yy or Zz

**Phonics** Draw a line from the Yy to pictures whose names begin with that letter sound.

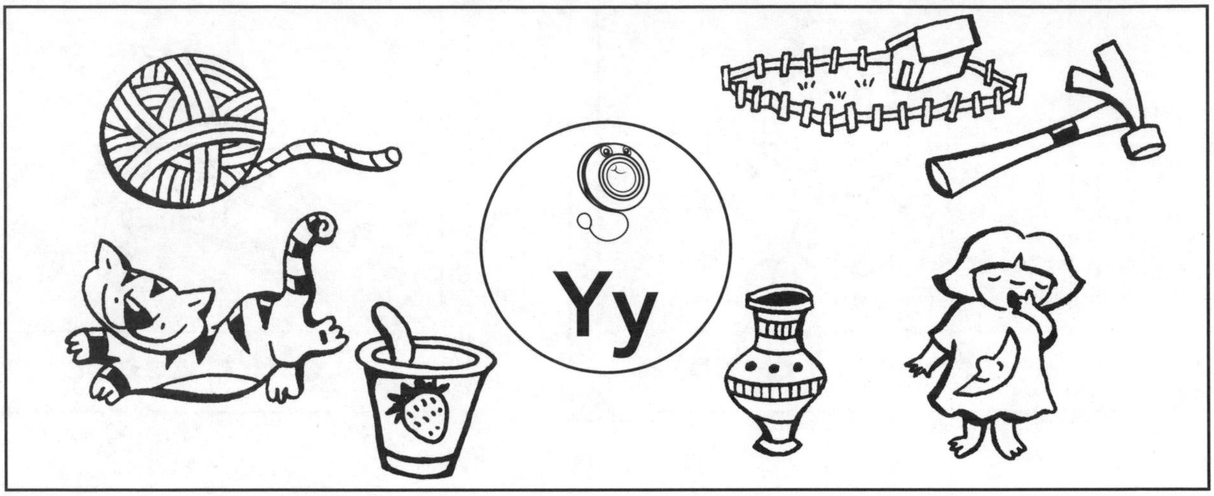


**Phonics** Draw a line from the Zz to pictures whose names begin with that letter sound.

**Word Play** Name the picture. Print the letter that begins the picture name.

z g i

Name ______________________________

# Ends with *s*

Name each picture. Color the pictures whose names have the same ending sound as  .

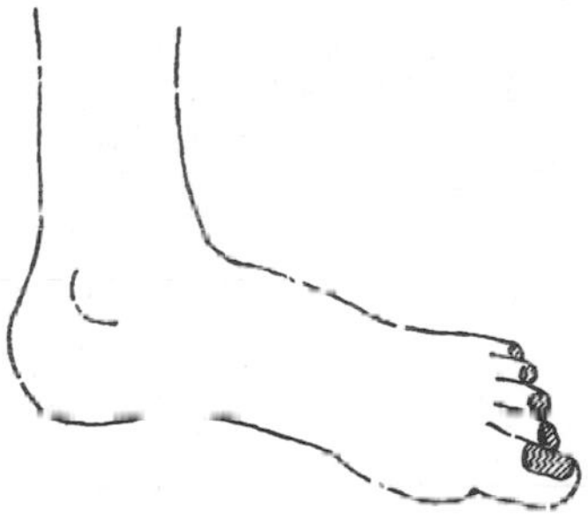

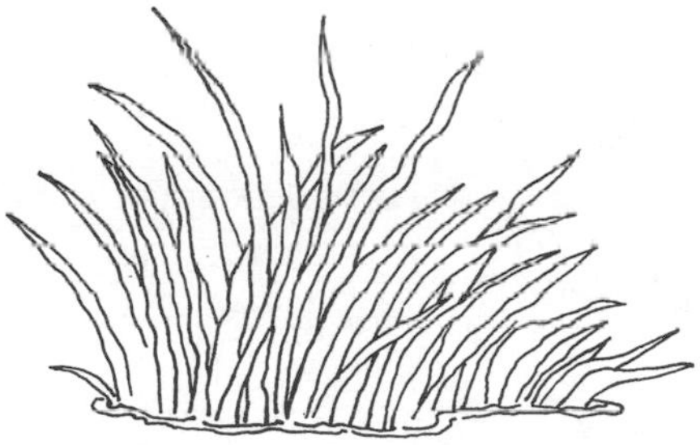
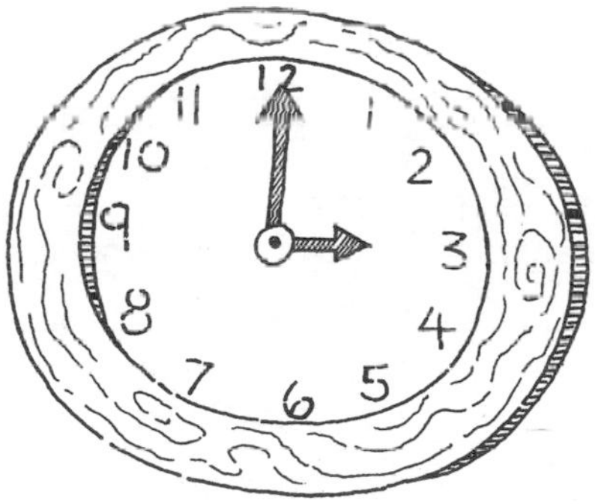

Name ____________________________________

# Ends with *t*

**Name each picture. Color the pictures whose names have the same ending sound as**  **.**

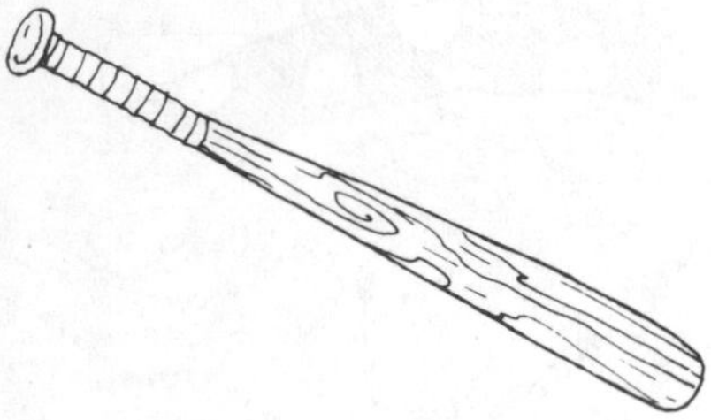

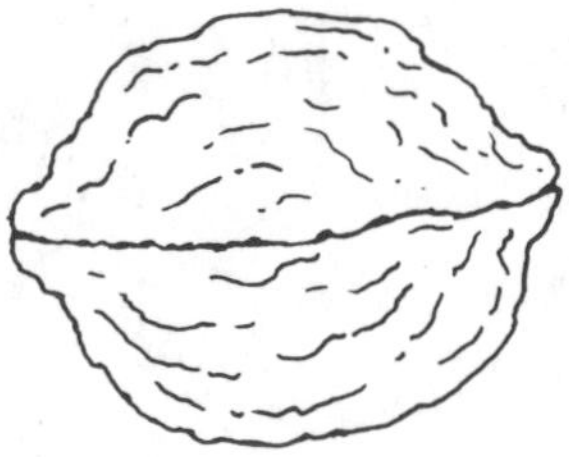

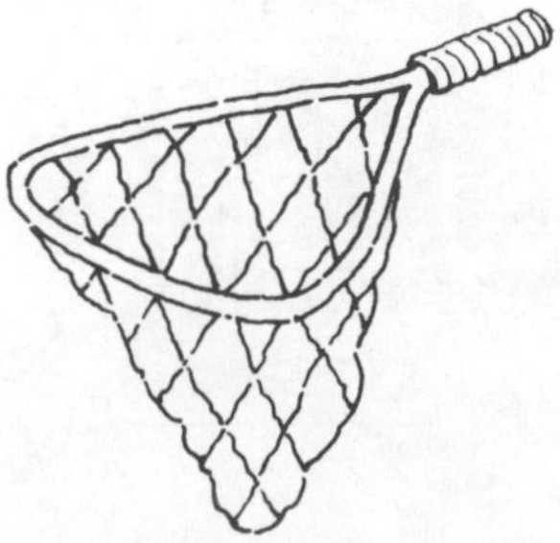

Name ____________________

# Begins with *m* or *s*

**Think of each beginning sound.**
**Write m or s.**

**m s**

1. ________

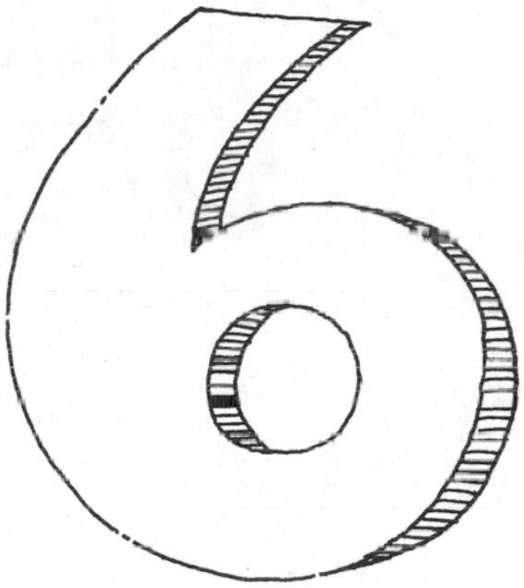

2. ________

3. ________

4. ________

5. ________

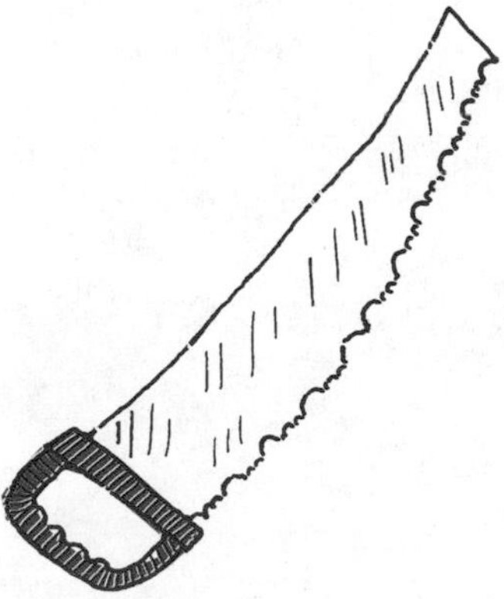

6. ________

Week 2

Phonics Final *n*

Name ______________________________

# Ends with *n*

**Name each picture. Color the pictures whose names have the same ending sound as  .**

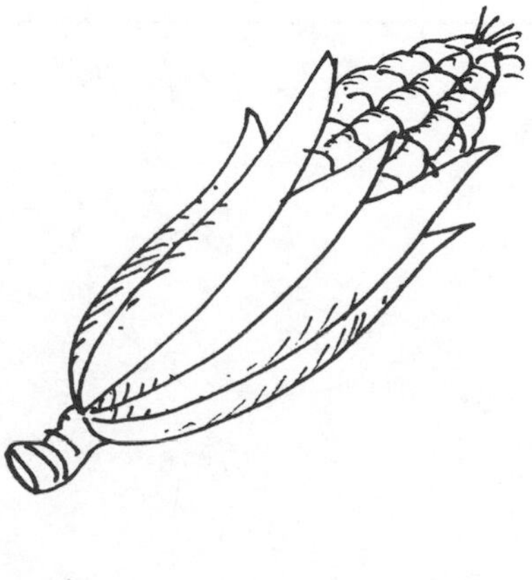

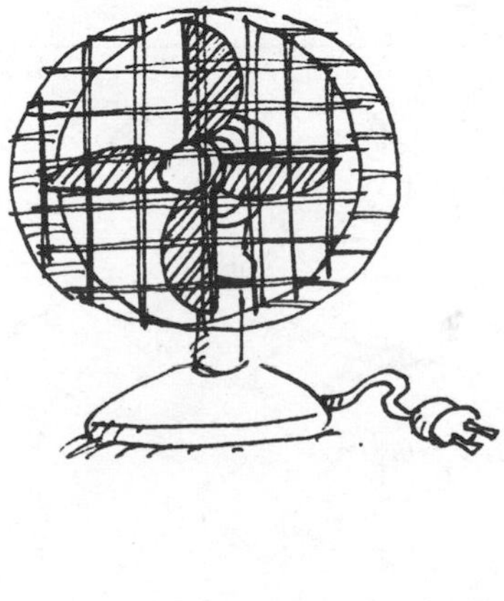

Name ______________________________

# Ends with *f*

**Name each picture. Color the pictures whose names have the same ending sound as**  **.**

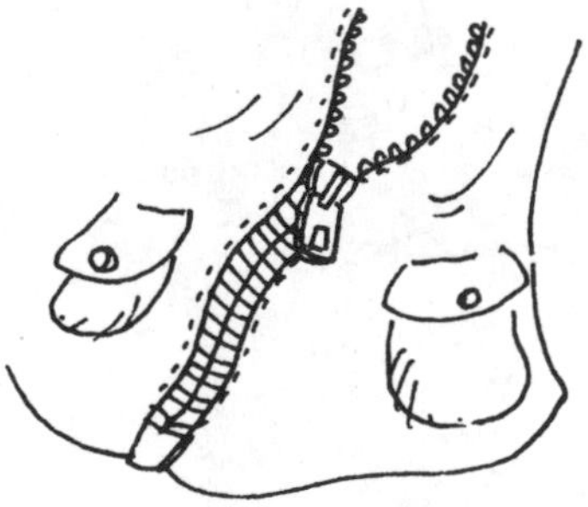

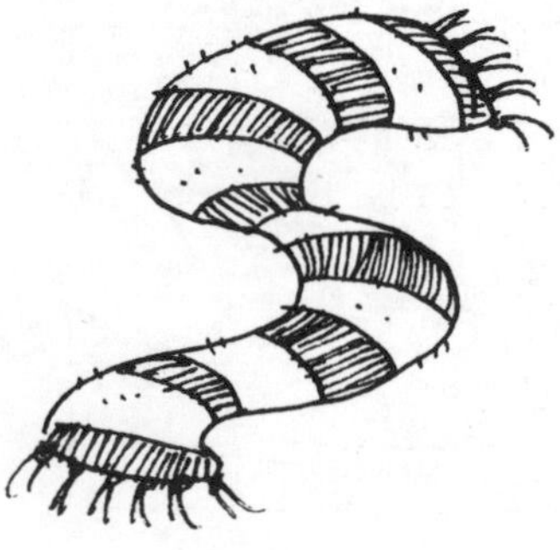

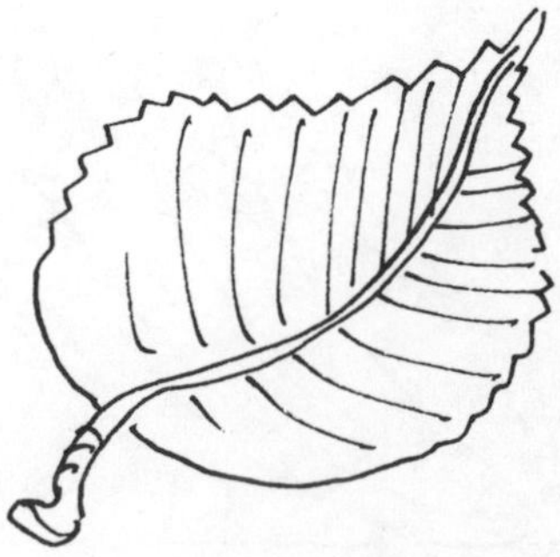

Name ________________________________

# Words with Short *a*

**Read the words in each box. Draw a line from the correct word to the picture.**

| | |
|---|---|
| cat<br><br>cap | fat<br><br>fan |
| pan<br><br>pat | mat<br><br>man |
| cat<br><br>cap | Pam<br><br>pan |
| cat<br><br>can | pat<br>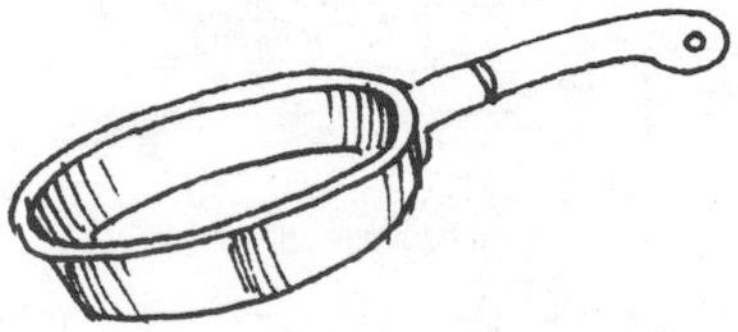<br>pan |

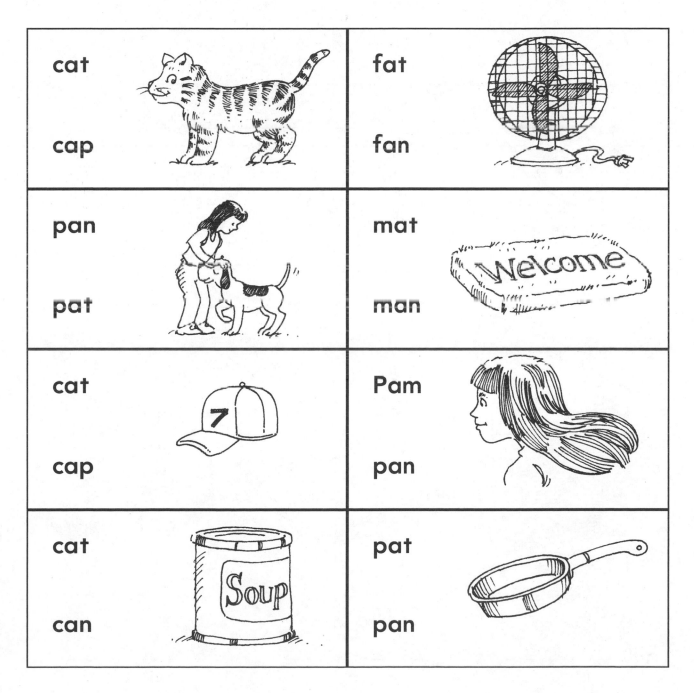

Name ______________________________

# Begins with *n* or *f*

**Think of each beginning sound.**

**Write n or f.**

**n f**

1. ______

2. ______

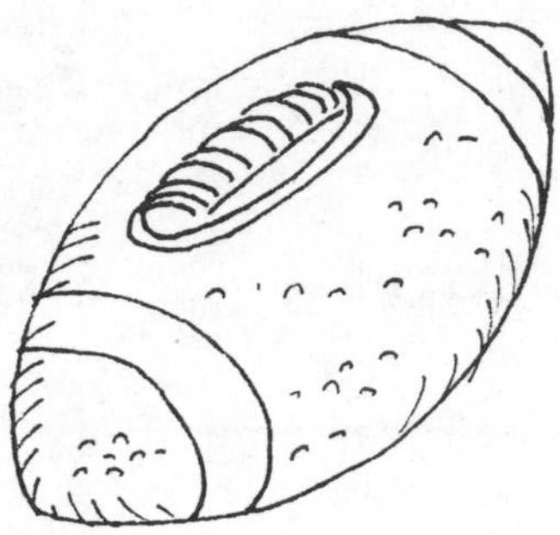

3. ______

4. ______

5. ______

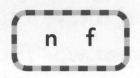

6. ______

Name ____________________________________

# Words to Know

Cut out and paste each sentence next to the picture it matches.

1. [ ]

2. [ ]

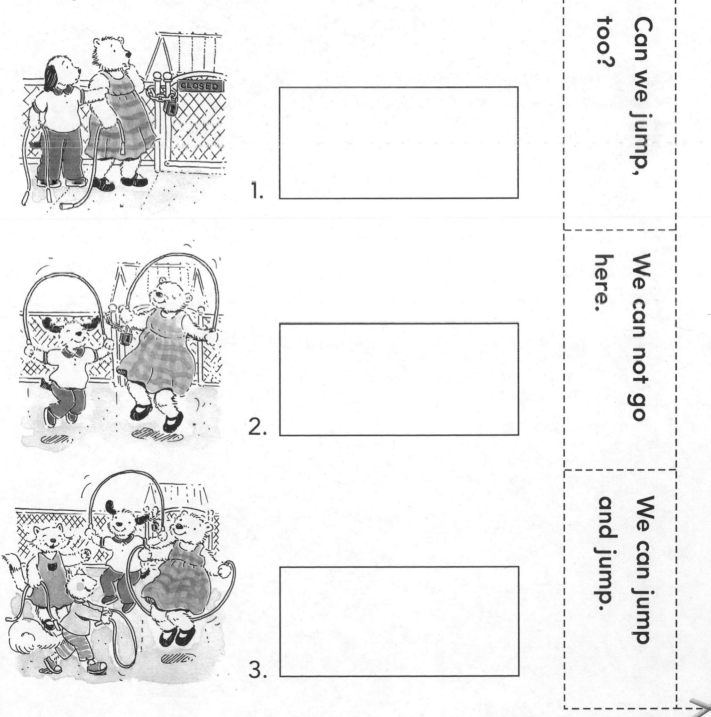

3. [ ]

Can we jump, too?

We can not go here.

We can jump and jump.

Name ______________________________

# Things We Do at School

Write and draw about something you do at school.

Cut out your sentence and picture.

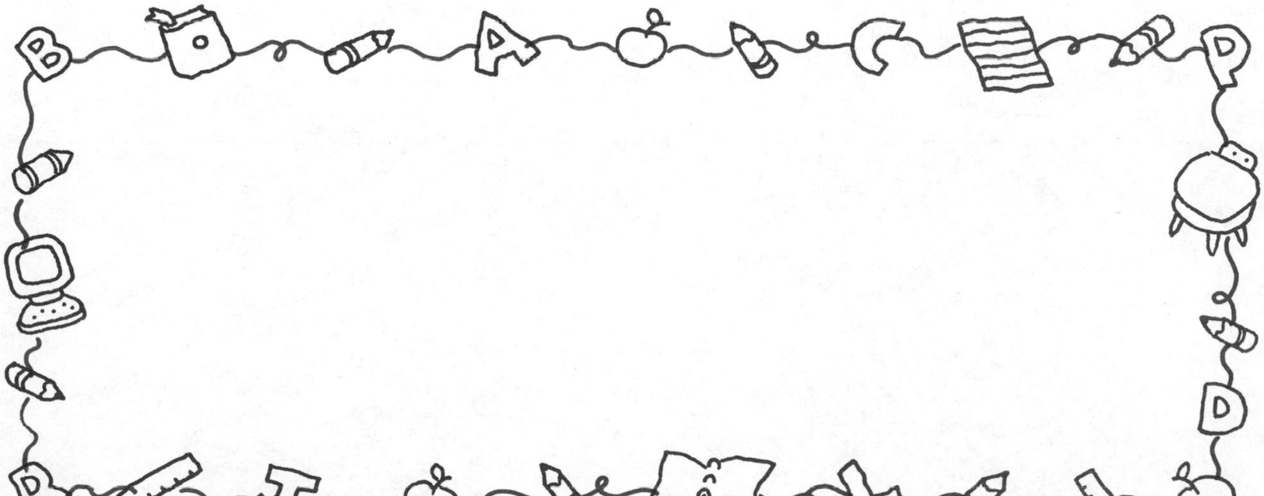

Name ______________________________

# Begins with *b*, *g*, *h*, *r*

**Name each picture. Circle the letter that stands for the beginning sound.**

| | | | |
|---|---|---|---|
| 1. <br>b r g | 2. <br>h r g | 3. <br>b g h | 4. <br>r g h |
| 5. <br>b r g | 6. <br>b r g | 7. <br>h r g | 8. <br>b r g |
| 9. <br>b g h | 10. 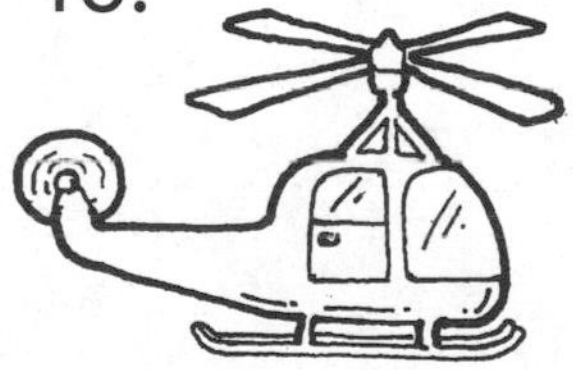<br>r g h | 11. <br>b g h | 12. <br>b r h |
| 13. <br>b r h | 14. <br>b r g | 15. 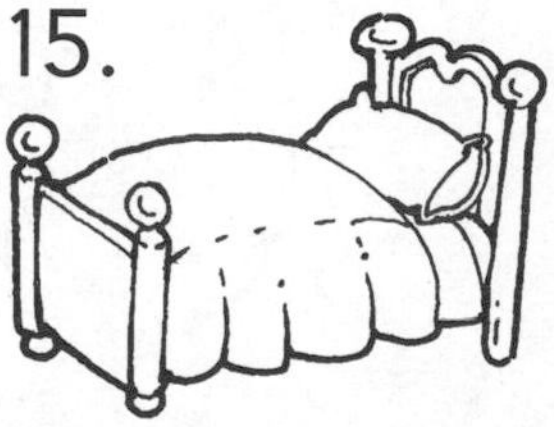<br>b r h | 16. <br>r g h |

Name ______________________________

# Ends with *b*

**Name each picture. Color the pictures whose names have the same ending sound as**  **.**

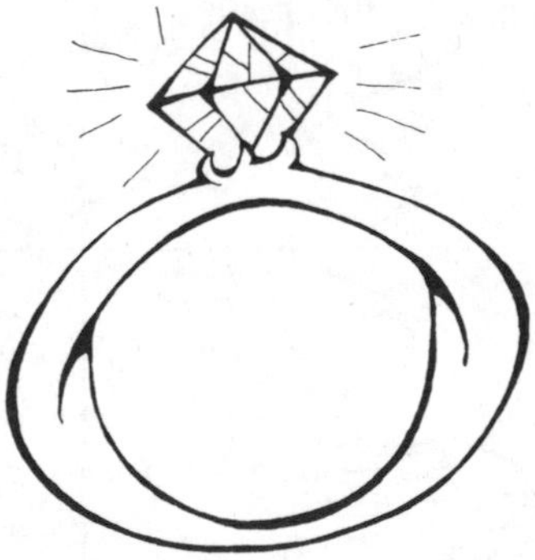

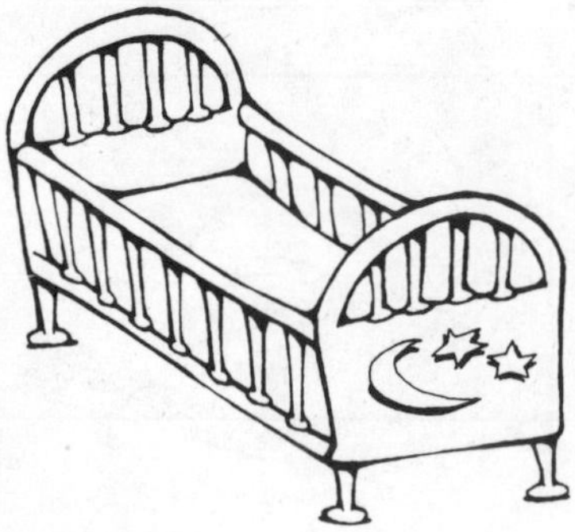

Name ______________________

# Ends with *g*

**Name each picture. Color the pictures whose names have the same ending sound as**  **.**

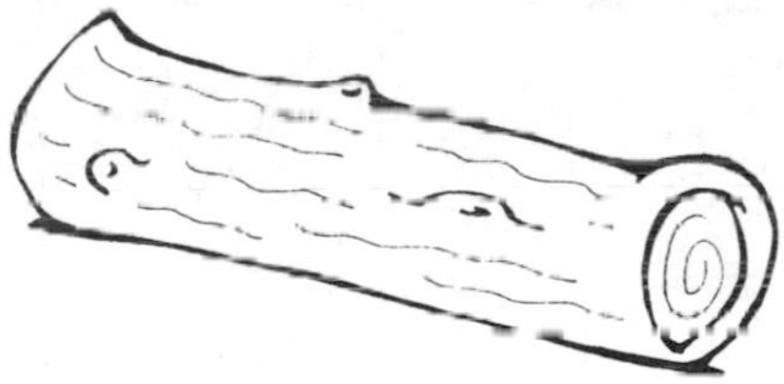

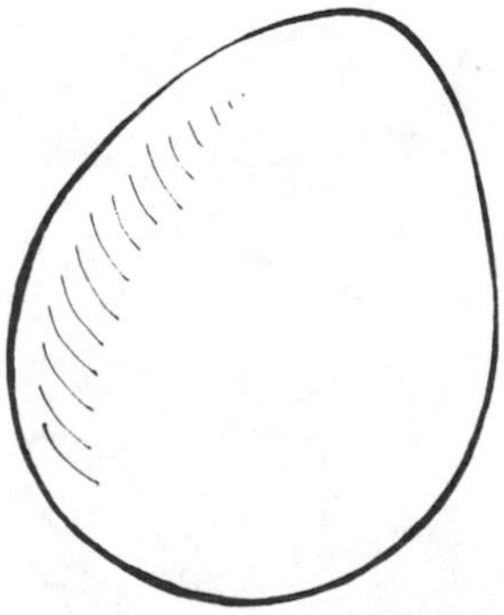

Name ______________________________

# Ends with *r*

**Name each picture. Color the pictures whose names have the same ending sound as**  **.**

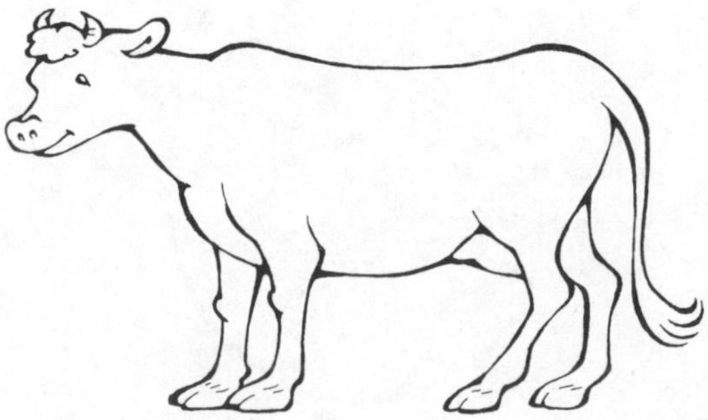

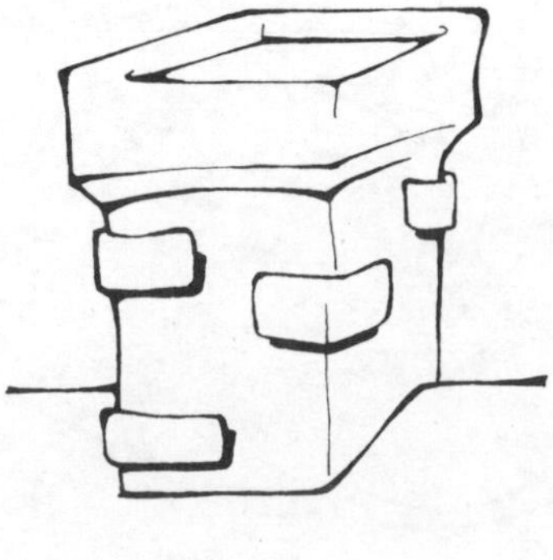

Week 3

**Phonics** Comparing Short Vowels

Name ______________________________

# Short *a* and *i*

**Read the words in each box. Draw a line from the correct word to the picture.**

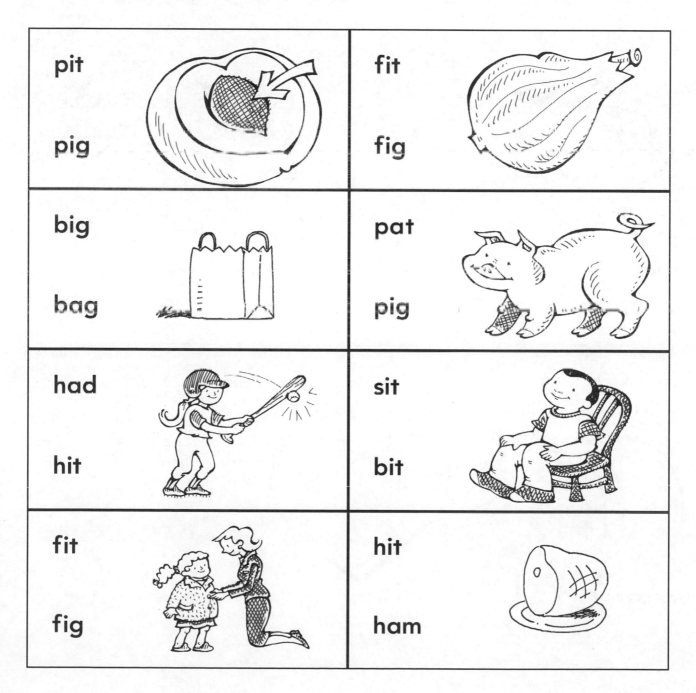

| | |
|---|---|
| pit 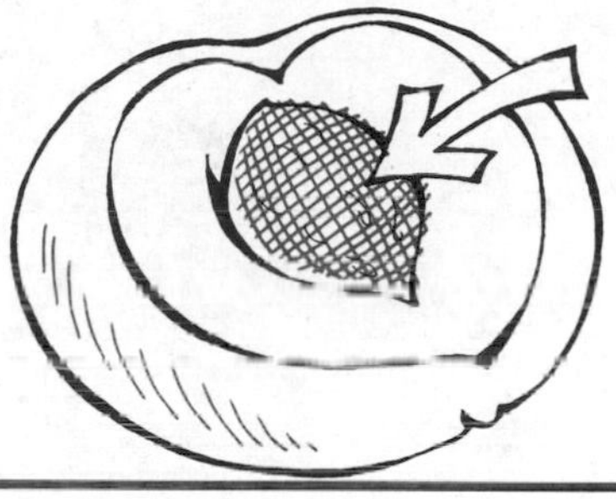 pig | fit 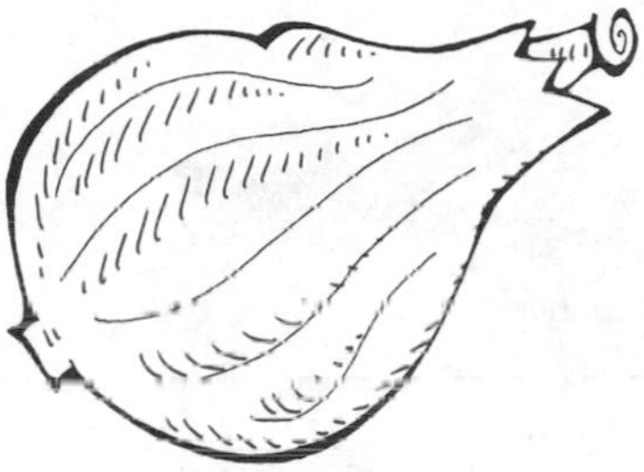 fig |
| big  bag | pat  pig |
| had  hit | sit  bit |
| fit  fig | hit 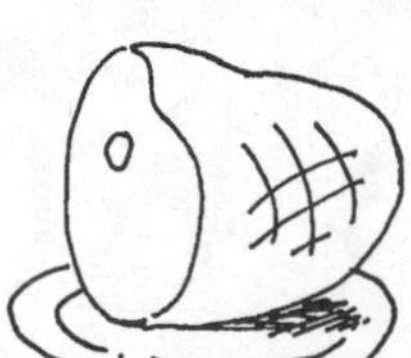 ham |

Name ________________________

# Begins with *b* or *h*

**Think of each beginning sound.**
**Write b or h.**

| b | h |
|---|---|

1. ______

2. ______

3. ______

4. ______

5. ______

6. ______

Name ______________________________

# What Happened?

Look at each picture. Draw a line from the picture of what happened to the picture showing why it happened.

| What happened? | Why? |
| --- | --- |
| 1.  |  |
| 2.  |  |
| 3.  |  |

Name ______________________

# Words to Know

Write a word from the box to complete each sentence.

**Word Bank**

find have who

1. Can Pat ____________ Nan?

2. We ____________ one pig and a cat.

3. ____________ can go to the mat?

Name ______________________________

# Words to Know

**Cut out and paste each sentence next to the picture it matches.**

1. [ ]

2. [ ]

a [ ]

Who can find the bat?

Who can jump to the hat?

We have one cat and a pig.

Name ______________________________

# Begins with *r* or *g*

Think of each beginning sound.
Write r or g.

r g

1. ________

2. ________

3. ________

4. ________

5. ________

6. ________

Week 3

Comprehension Check
*The Big Hit*

Name ________________________________

# Who Can Hit?

Read each sentence. Draw a line from the picture to the sentence that tells about it.

1.

We have a big bat.

Sam can hit.

---

2.

Go, Sam, go!

Pat can hit, too.

---

3.

Nat hit one big hit.

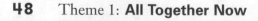

We ran, ran, ran!

Name ______________________

# At the Farm

Write a word from the box to complete each sentence.

**Word Bank**

carrot farm feed

1. Nan can go to the ______________ !

2. Big Pig can have a ______________ .

3. The man can ______________ Big Pig.

Name ______________________________

# Big Pig's Farm

Write **Nan, Tim,** or **Big Pig** to tell about each character in the story **Big Pig.**

1. The big hat can fit

   ______________________________ .

2. ______________________________ can feed Big Pig a fig.

3. ______________________________ can feed Big Pig a carrot.

4. ______________________________ can go!

Name ____________________

# My Own Ending

**Draw a new ending for Big Pig.**

Name ______________________________

# Begins with *d*, *w*, *l*, or *x*

**Name each picture. Circle the letter that stands for the beginning sound.**

| | | | |
|---|---|---|---|
| 1. 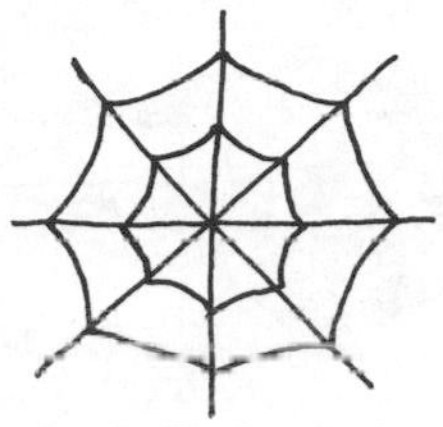 d w l | 2.  d l x | 3. 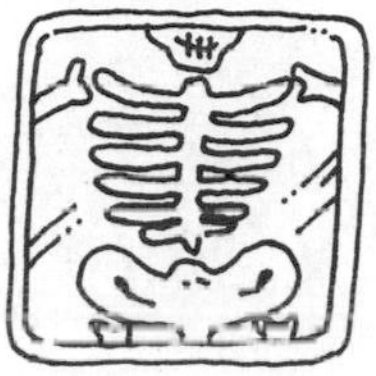 w x d | 4.  x l d |
| 5.  l x w | 6. 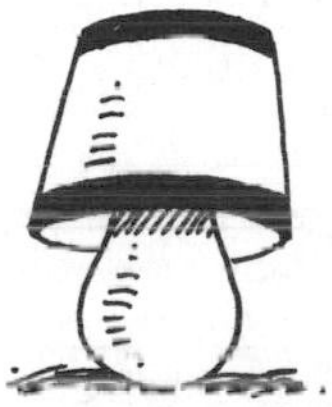 w l d | 7. 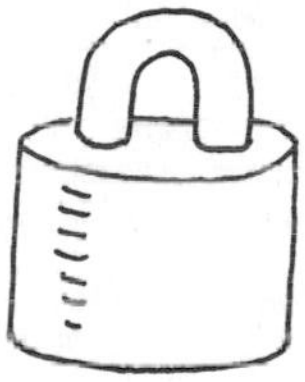 d w l | 8.  l d w |
| 9. 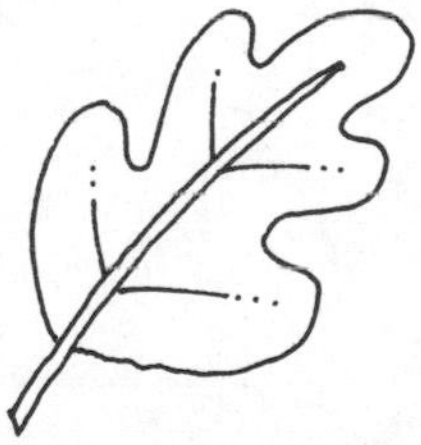 w d l | 10.  d l w | 11.  d x w | 12.  l d w |
| 13. 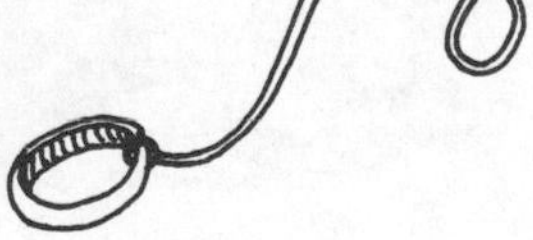 d x l | 14.  l d w | 15. 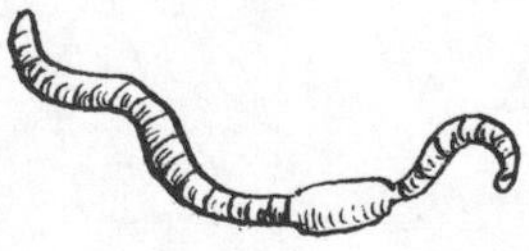 w x d | 16.  w d l |

Name ______________________

# Ends with *d*

Name each picture. Write **d** if the word ends like **Ted**. Then draw a line from Ted to his bed.

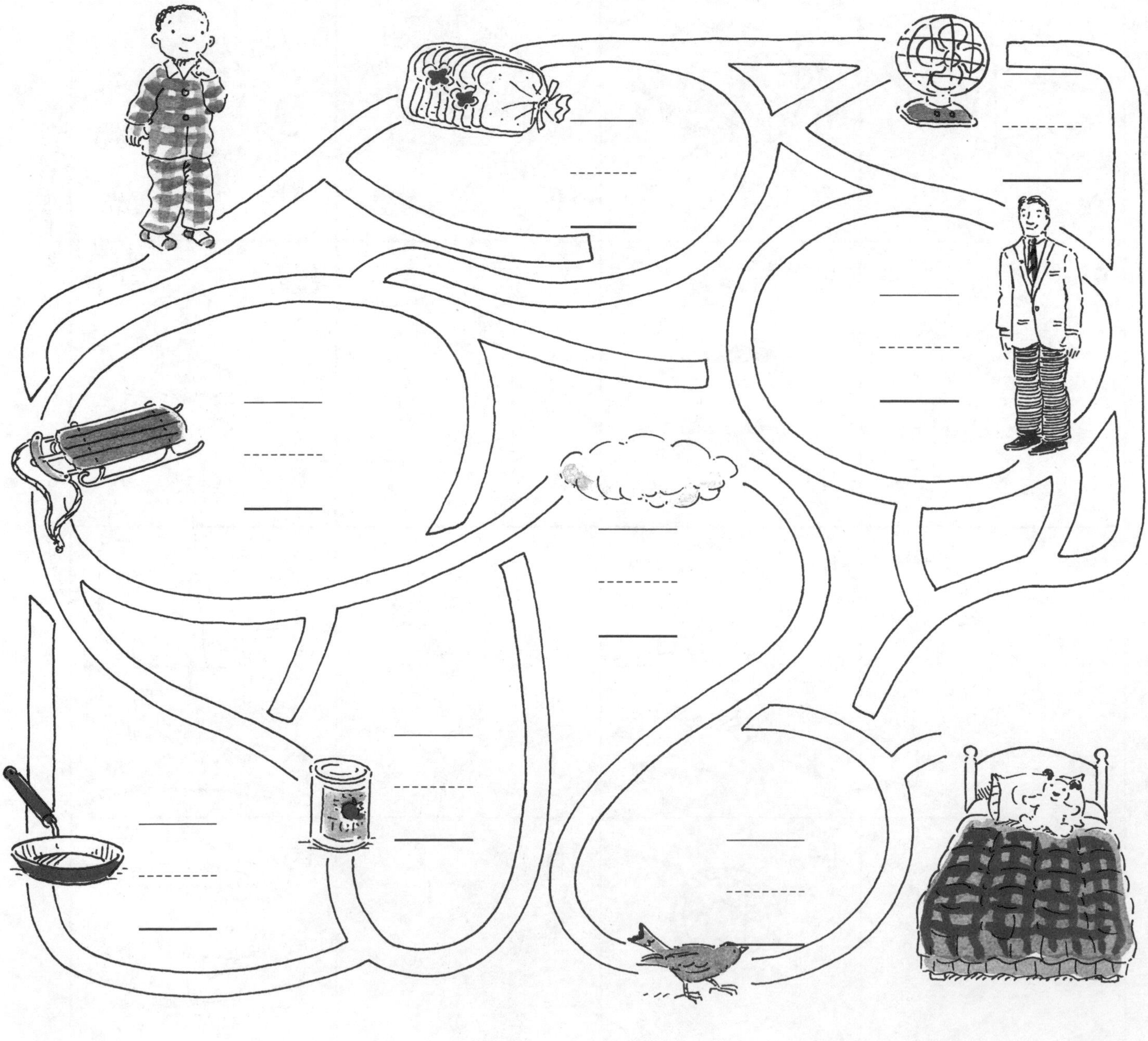

Name ______________________________

# Ends with *l*

**Name each picture. Color the pictures whose names have the same ending sound as owl.**

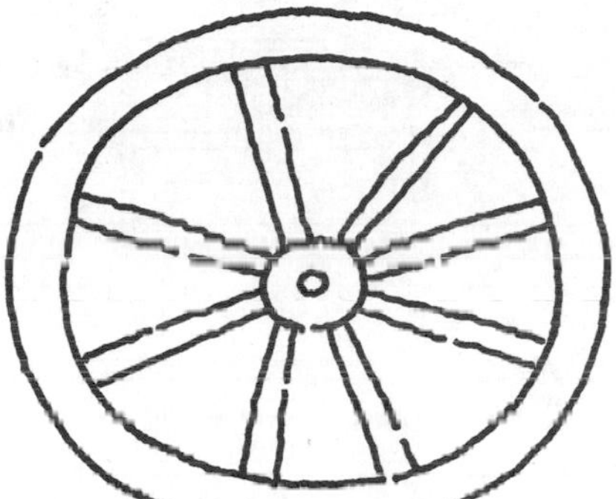

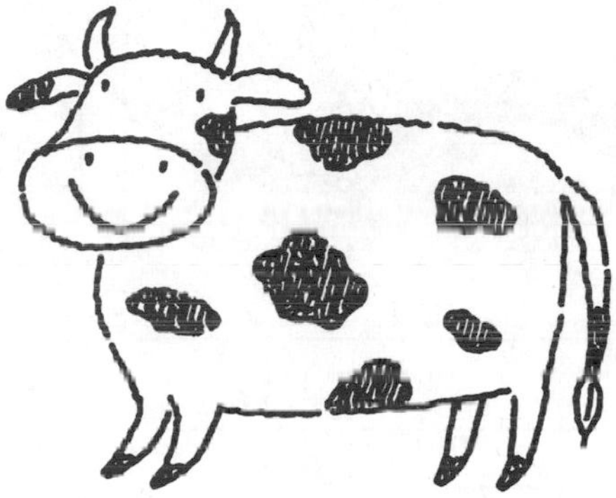

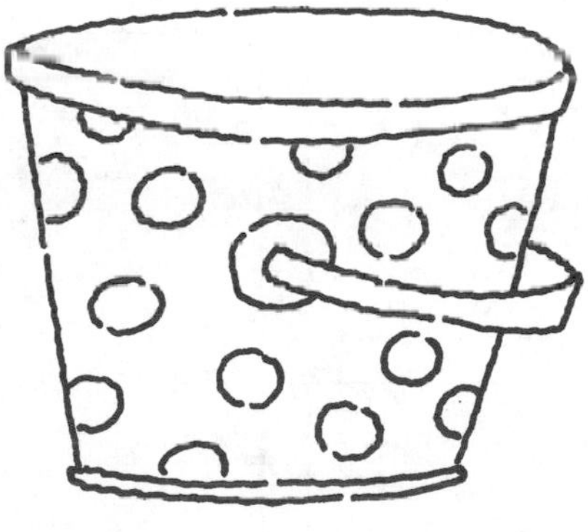
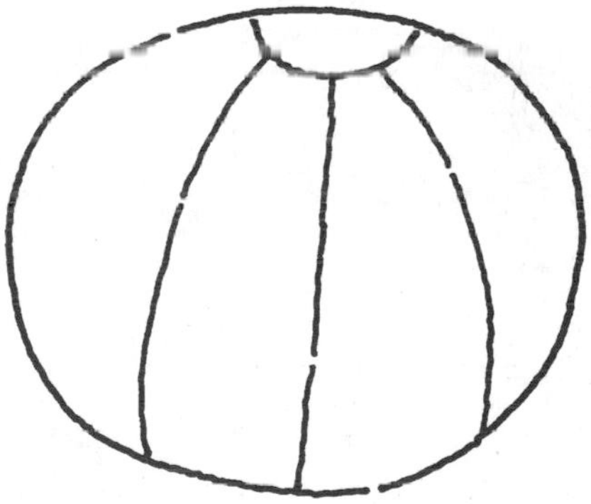

Name ______________________________

# Ends with *x*

**Name each picture. Write x if the word ends like mix. Then draw a line from the fox to his box.**

Week 1

**Phonics** Blending Short *o* Words

Name ______________________

# Blending Short *o* Words

Blend the letter sounds. Then write the correct word for each picture.

| h | o | t |
|---|---|---|

| b | o | x |
|---|---|---|

| m | o | p |
|---|---|---|

| d | o | t |
|---|---|---|

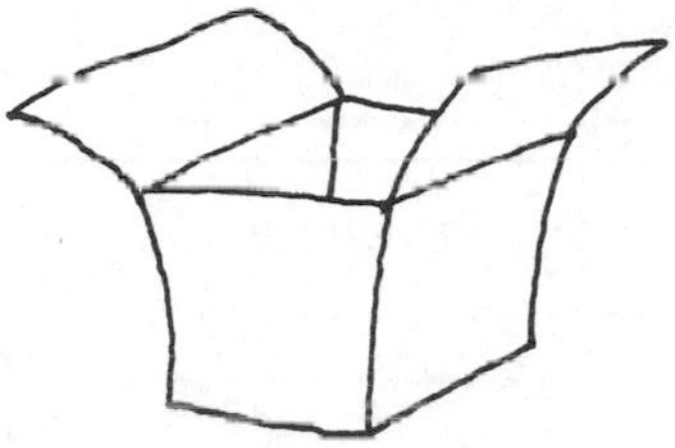

______________________ ______________________

______________________ ______________________

Name ______________________

# Words with Short *o*

Write a word from the box to complete each sentence.

**Word Bank**

on fox box

1. Go, __________, go!

2. The fox sat __________ the ox.

3. The ox sat on the __________ !

Name ______________________________

# Short *a*, *i*, and *o*

**Write a word from the box to name each picture.**

**Word Bank**

map pig pot dog pat mop

1. 

2. 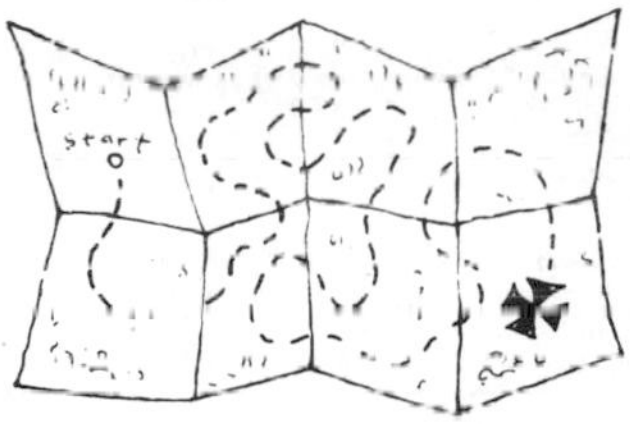

3. 

4. 

5. 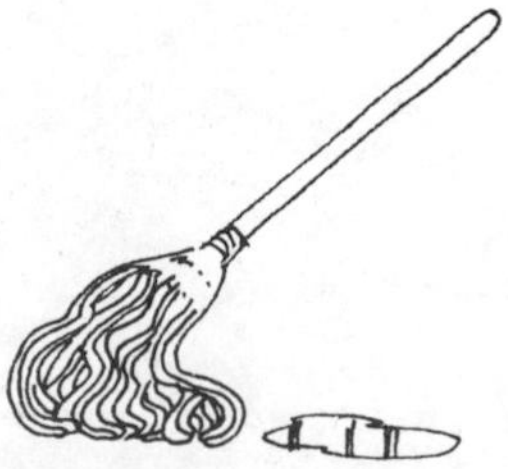

6. 

Name ______________________________

# Begins with *d* or *l*

**Name each picture. Think of the beginning sound. Write d or l.**

**d l**

| | | |
|---|---|---|
| 1.  ___ | 2.  ___ | 3. 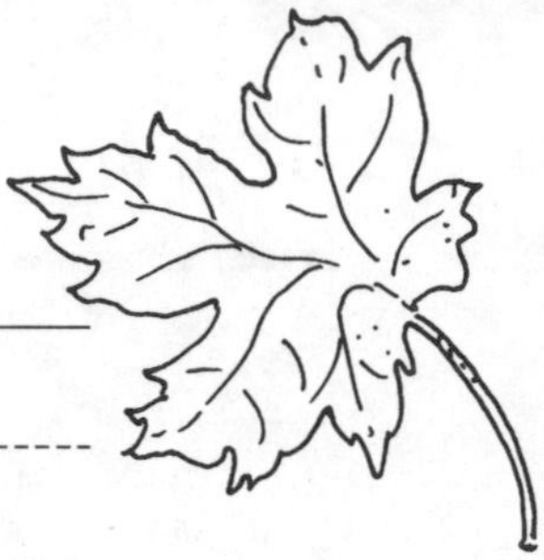 ___ |
| 4.  ___ | 5. 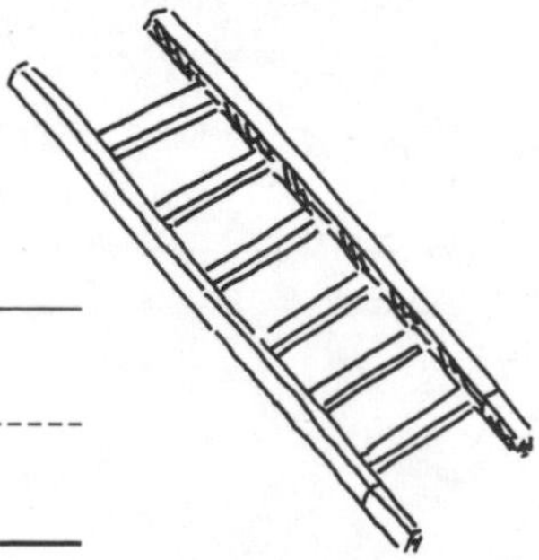 ___ | 6. 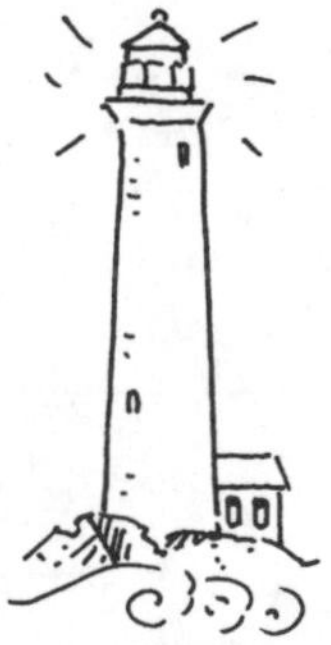 ___ |
| 7.  ___ | 8.  ___ | 9. 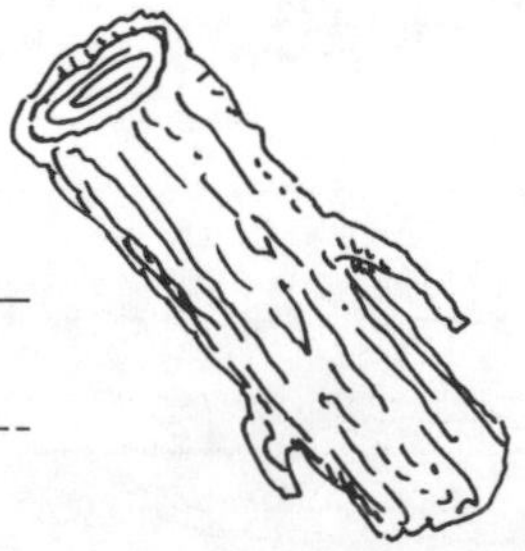 ___ |
| 10.  ___ | 11.  ___ | 12.   ___ |

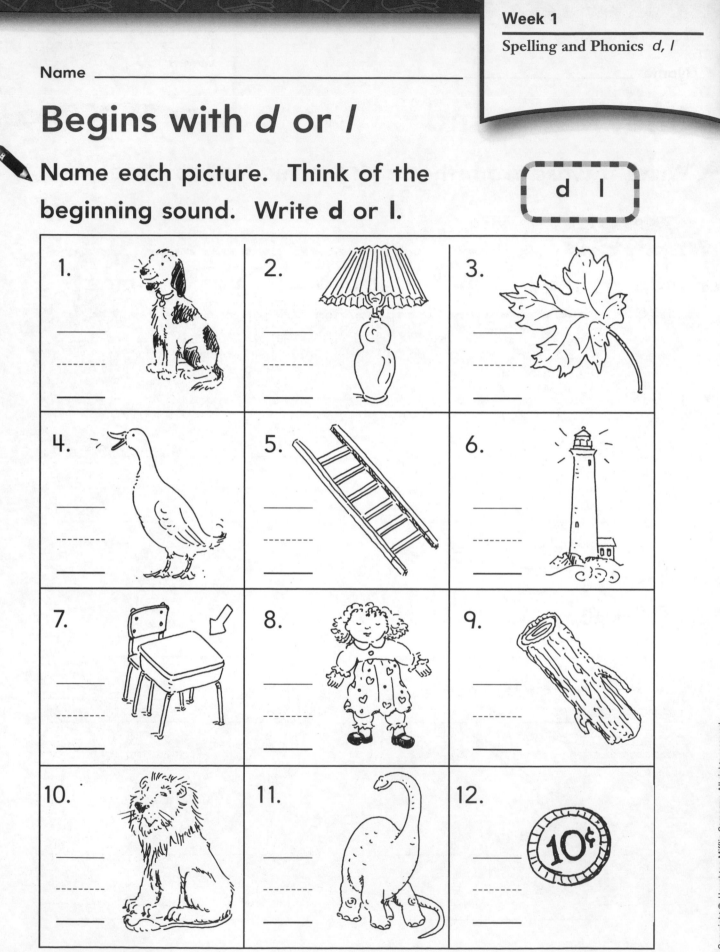

Week 1

Comprehension Noting Details

Name ______________________________

# Who Can Find It?

Read each sentence. Follow the directions.

Color a cat with one bat.

Color an ox in a big hat.

Name ______________________________

# Words to Know

Draw a line from each story to each picture that shows what the story is about.

1. What have we here?
We have one, two, three.
We have four and five!

2. A cat can sit.
It can sit upon a box.
It can sit in the box, too.

3. Can the cat fit in?
It fit in the box once.
The cat got too big!

Name ______________________

# Words to Know

Circle the sentence that tells about each picture.

1. One cat sat upon a box.

   We jump here.

2. Five sit.

   Three have hats.

3. A man can bat.

   Once, the four wigs fit in here.

4. What can we find?

   We have a big pan.

Name ______________________________

# Words with *w* or *x*

**Name each picture. Circle the pictures whose names begin with w. Write w if the word begins with w.**

1. ________

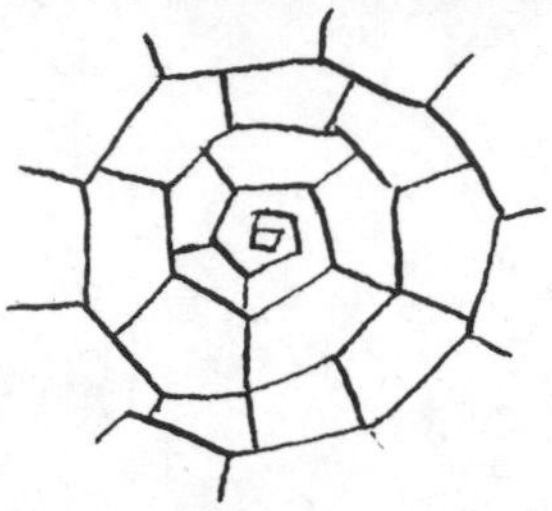

2. ________

3. ________

4. ________

5. ________

6. ________

**Write x to complete each word. Draw a picture for each word.**

fo ____

bo ____

Name ____________________________

# What's in the Box?

Read each sentence. Draw a line from each picture to the sentence that tells about it.

1. 

2. 

3. 

4. 

5. 

6. 

A fox can fit in the box.

A pig can fit, too.

A hat can fit in the box.

Dot got the box.

Dan and Dot can fit, too.

Dot can find a lot in the box.

Name ______________________________

# Wigs, Wigs, Wigs!

**Write a word from the box to complete each sentence.**

**Word Bank**

| | | | | |
|---|---|---|---|---|
| ball | thanks | shelf | win | wigs |

1. What can Nat Cat ____________ ?

2. What is on the ____________ ?

3. Can Nat Cat win ____________ ?

4. Get a ____________ , Nat Cat.

5. ____________ , Dot Dog!

Name ______________________________

# About the Story

**Circle the picture that answers each question.**

1. **Who can hit the ball in?**

2. **What can Pat Pig win?**

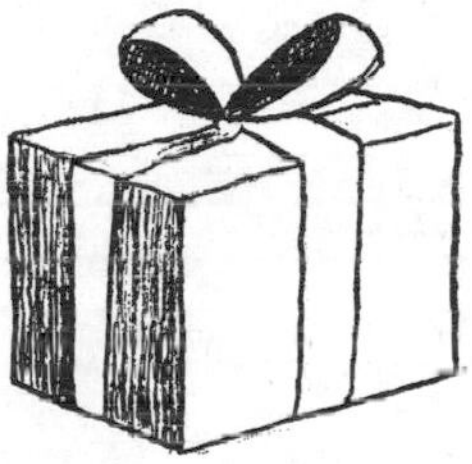

3. **What can Pat Pig find in the box?**

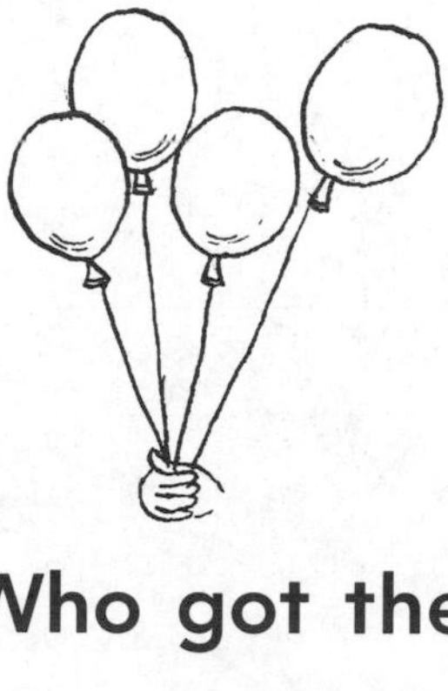
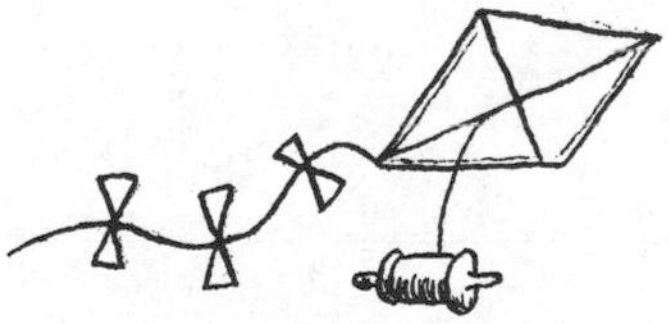

4. **Who got the thanks?**

Name ______________________________

# Begins the Same

Cut out and paste each word next to the animal whose name begins with the same sound.

1. 

2. 

3. 

4. 

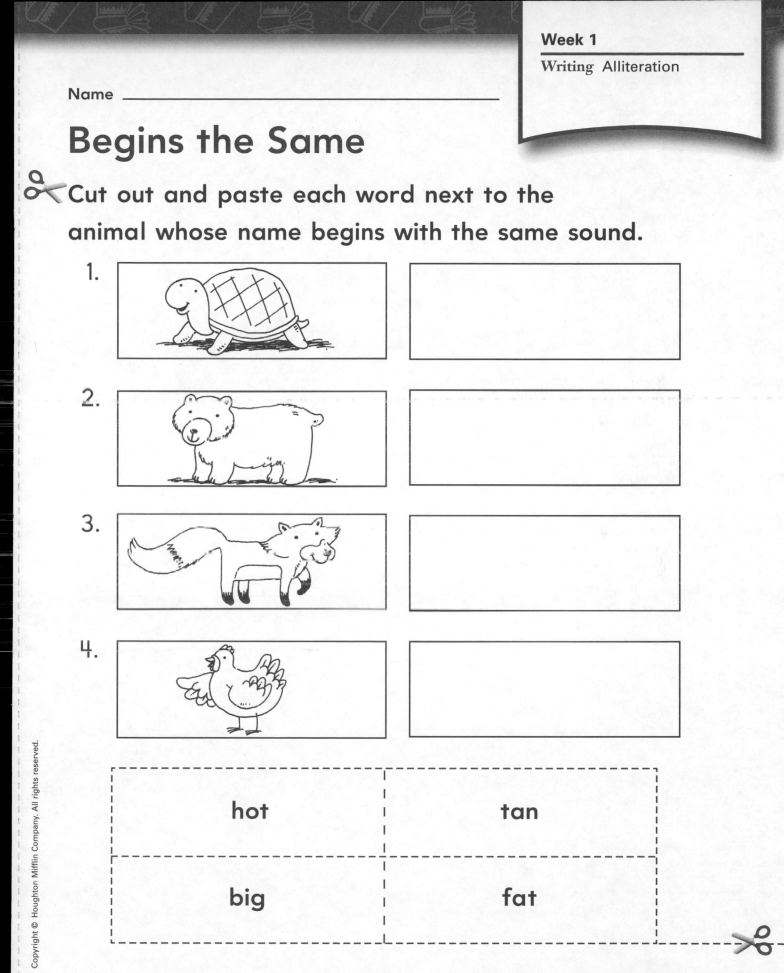

| | |
|---|---|
| hot | tan |
| big | fat |

Name ______________________________

# Begins with *y, k,* or *v*

**Name each picture. Circle the letter that stands for the beginning sound.**

| | | | |
|---|---|---|---|
| 1.  y v k | 2.  k v y | 3.  y v k | 4.  v y k |
| 5.  k v y | 6. 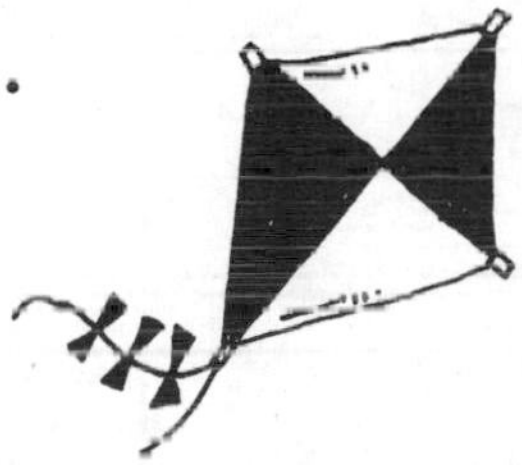 k y v | 7.  k v y | 8.  y v k |
| 9. 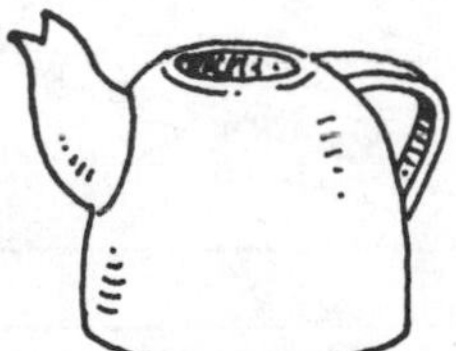 v y k | 10.  k v y | 11. 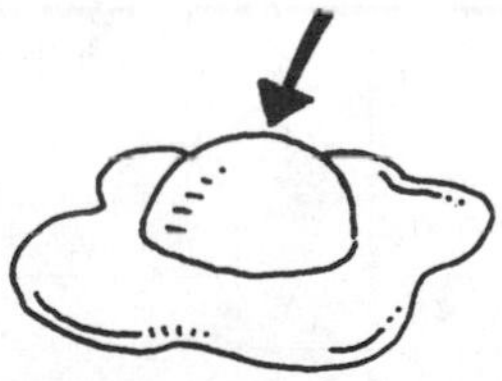 k y v | 12.  y k v |
| 13.  k y v | 14.  k v y | 15.  k y v | 16.  y k v |

Name ______________________________

# Ends with *k*

**Name each picture. Write k if the word ends like look. Write g if the word ends like big.**

**k g**

1. 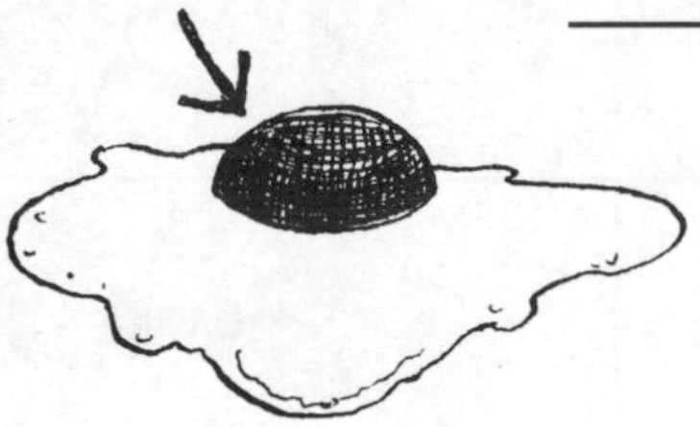

2. 

3. 

4. 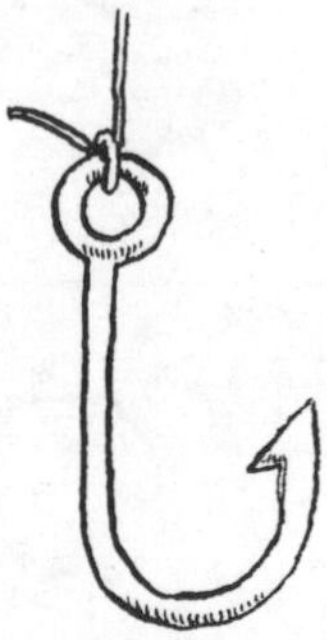

5. 

6. 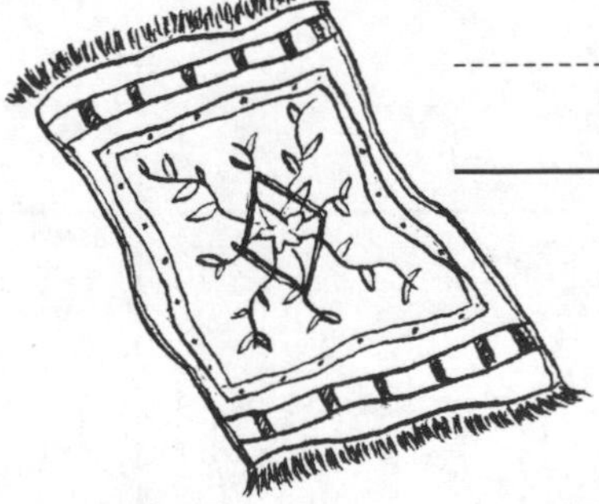

7. 

8. 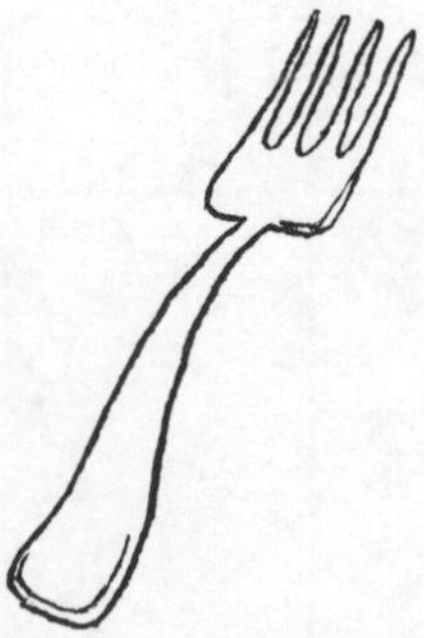

9. 

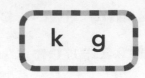

Name ______________________________

# Blending Short *e* Words

Blend the letter sounds. Then write the correct word for each picture.

| w | e | b |
|---|---|---|

| b | e | d |
|---|---|---|

| n | e | t |
|---|---|---|

| t | e | n |
|---|---|---|

1. ______________________

2. ______________________

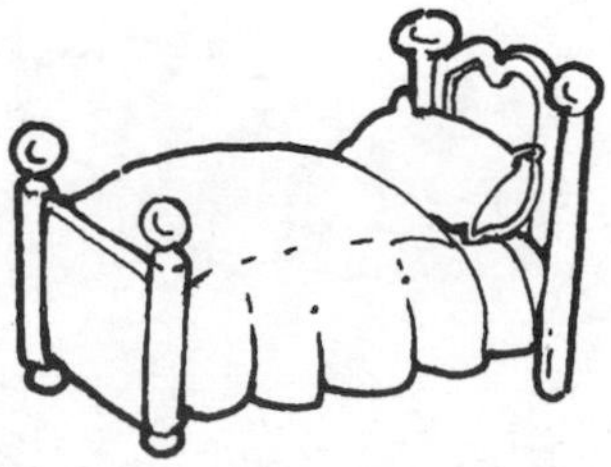

3. ______________________

4. ______________________

Name ______________________

# Words with Short *e*

Write a word from the box to complete each sentence.

**Word Bank**

| | | | |
|---|---|---|---|
| ten | bed | pet | get |

1. I am in ________ .

2. We can ________ a box.

3. The ________ jumps in.

4. We have ________ cats.

Name ______________________________

# Short *a*, *e*, *i*, and *o*

**Read the words in each box. Draw a line from the correct word to the picture.**

| | | | |
|---|---|---|---|
| pat<br>pot |  | met<br>men |  |
| wag<br>wig |  | pan<br>pen |  |
| ten<br>tan |  | hit<br>hen |  |
| dig<br>dog |  | vet<br>vat |  |

Name ______________________________

# Begins with *y* or *v*

**Name each picture. Think of the beginning sound. Write y or v.**

y v

| | | |
|---|---|---|
| 1.  | 2.  | 3. 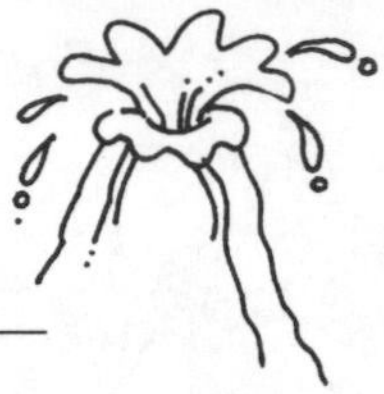 |
| 4. 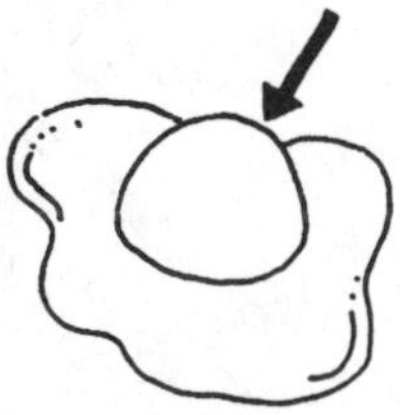 | 5.  | 6.  |
| 7.  | 8.  | 9. 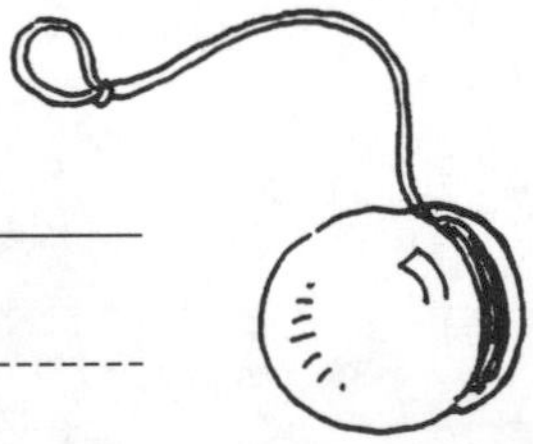 |
| 10.  | 11.  | 12.  |

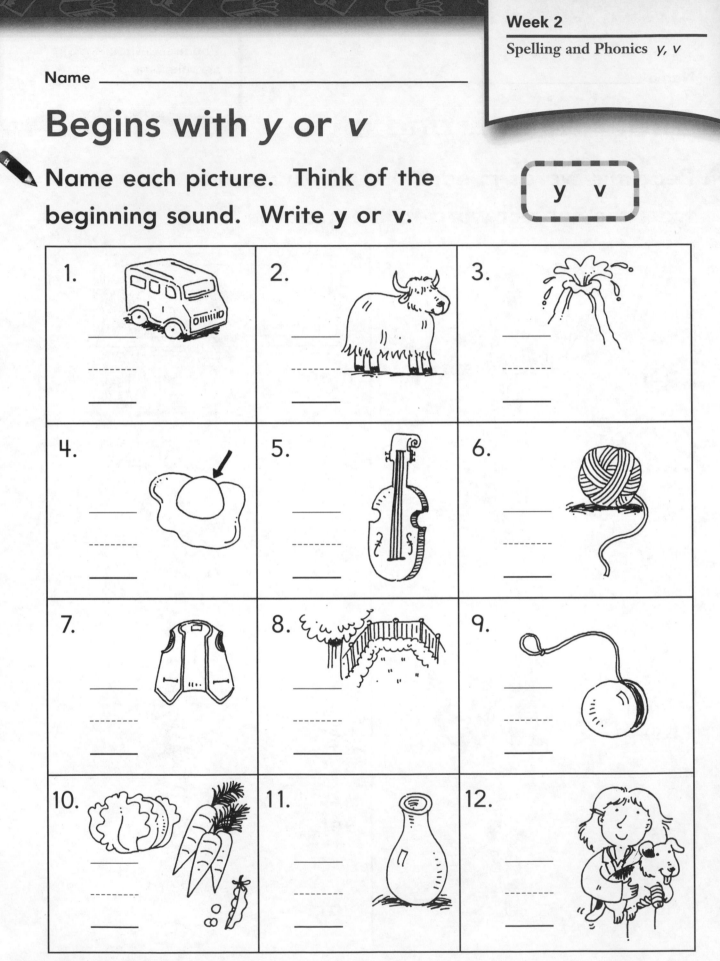

Name ______________________________

# Could It Really Happen?

Look at each picture. If the picture shows something that could really happen, color it.

Name ____________________

# Words to Know

Write a word from the box to complete each sentence in the story.

**Word Bank**

| | | | |
|---|---|---|---|
| I | my | for | do |

1. "I have ________ bat," said Van.

2. Dot said, "I ______ not have a bat."

3. Van said, "The bat is ________ me.
The bat is for you, too."

4. Dot said, " ___ can hit. You can hit, too."

Week 2

High-Frequency Words

Name ______________________

# Words to Know

Write a word from the box to complete each sentence in the story.

**Word Bank**

| | | | |
|---|---|---|---|
| me | is | said | you |

1. "What can I do for you?" ______________ the vet.

2. "My pet _______ here," I said.

3. "Can you get my pet for ______ ?" I said.

4. "Here __________ go," said the vet.

Name ______________________________

# Begins with *k*

**Name each picture. Color the pictures that have the same beginning sound as kit.**

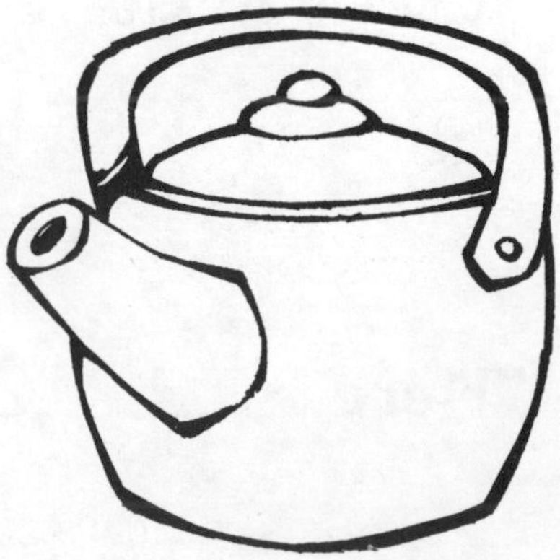

Name ____________________

# Vets Can Help

Read each question. Circle the correct answer.

1. Who is Big Ben?

   Big Ben is a pet cat.

   Big Ben is a pig.

2. Who can do a lot for Big Ben?

   Ken can do a lot.

   The vet can do a lot.

---

3. Who is in the pen?

   A big pet is in the pen.

   A cat is in the pen.

4. Who is in the van?

   Nan is in the van.

   The vet is in the van.

5. What can the vet do?

   The vet can do a lot for the big pet.

   The vet can get the hen in the pen.

Name ______________________

# Wanted: Soup!

Write a word from the box to complete each sentence in the story.

**Word Bank**

soup fire wanted vat noodle

1. Dan lit the ______________ .
2. Dan wanted hot ______________ soup.
3. Dan got a ______________ .
4. Pat ______________ noodle soup, too!
5. Pat and Dan can have hot ______________ .

Name ______________________________

# Put Them in Order!

Cut out and paste the sentences in the order that they happened in the story.

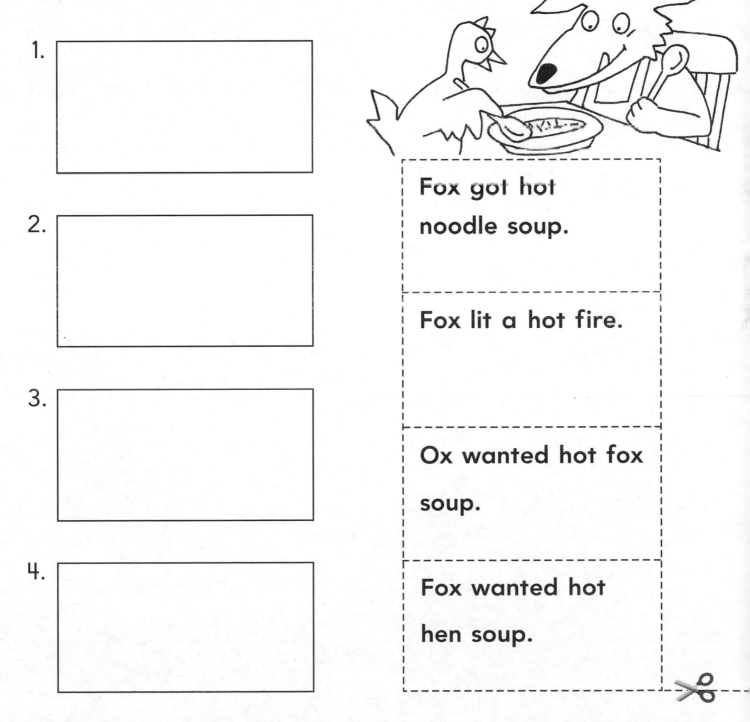

1. 

2. 

3. 

4. 

Fox got hot noodle soup.

Fox lit a hot fire.

Ox wanted hot fox soup.

Fox wanted hot hen soup.

Name ______________________

# An Animal Fact

Draw a picture of an animal.

Write about the animal.

My animal is ______________________ .

It can ______________________

______________________ .

Name ____________________



# Begins with *qu*, *j*, or *z*

**Name each picture. Circle the letter that stands for the beginning sound.**

| | | | |
|---|---|---|---|
| 1.  j qu z | 2.  z qu j | 3.  qu j z | 4.  j z qu |
| 5.  j z qu | 6.  j qu z | 7.  j z qu | 8.  qu j z |
| 9.  j qu z | 10.  z qu j | 11. 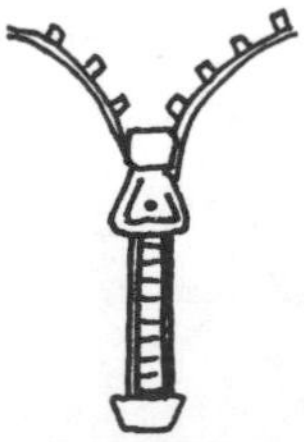 z j qu | 12.  z qu j |
| 13.  z j qu | 14.   z j qu | 15. 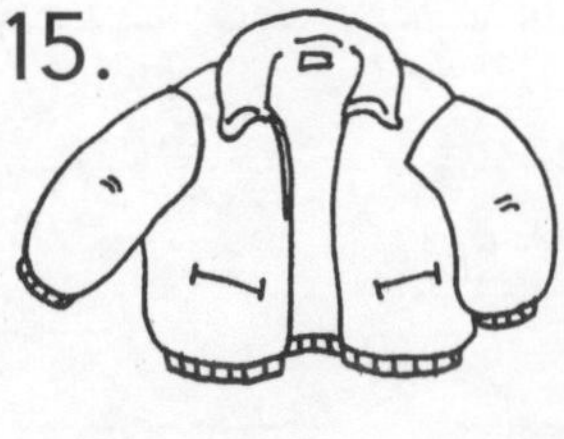 qu j z | 16. 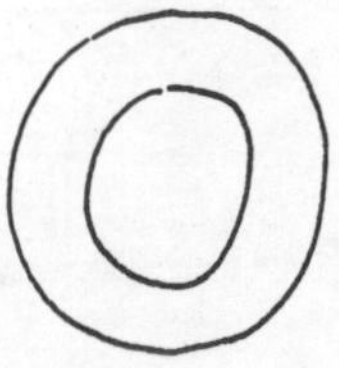 z qu j |

Week 3

Phonemic Awareness
Short *u*

Name ______________________________

# Short *u*

**Name each picture. Color the pictures whose names have the same vowel sound as**  **.**

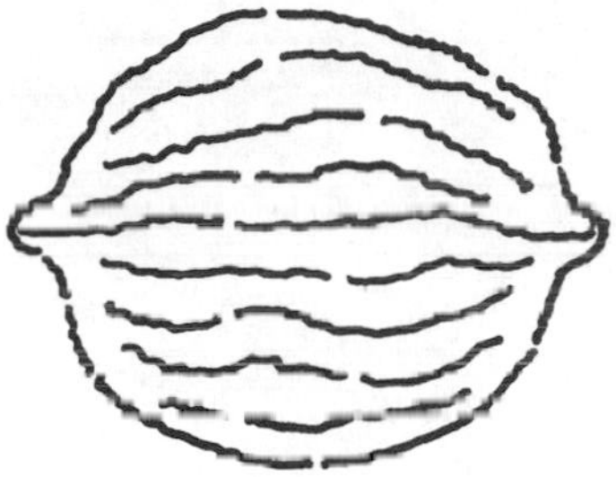
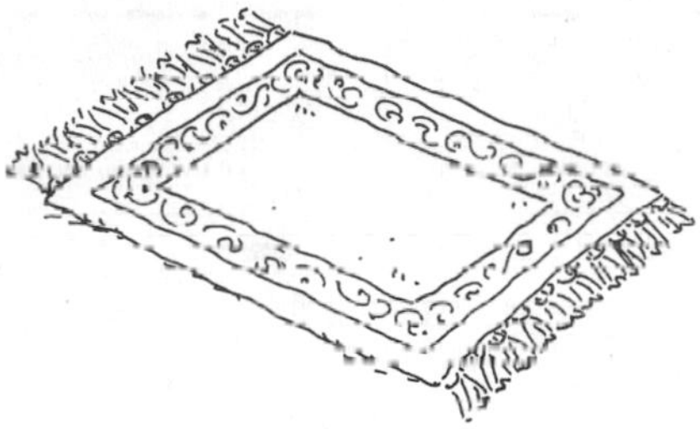
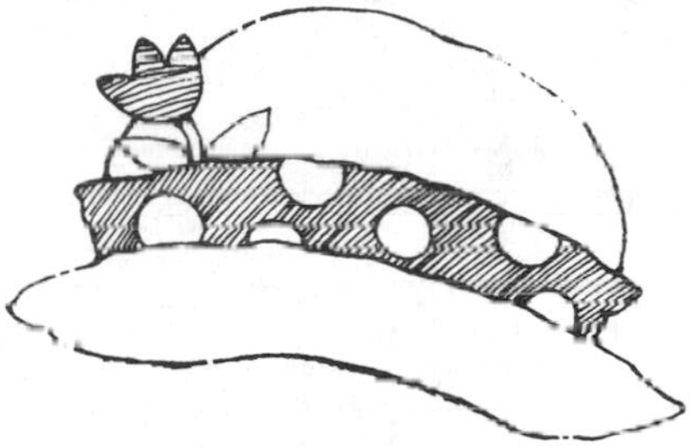

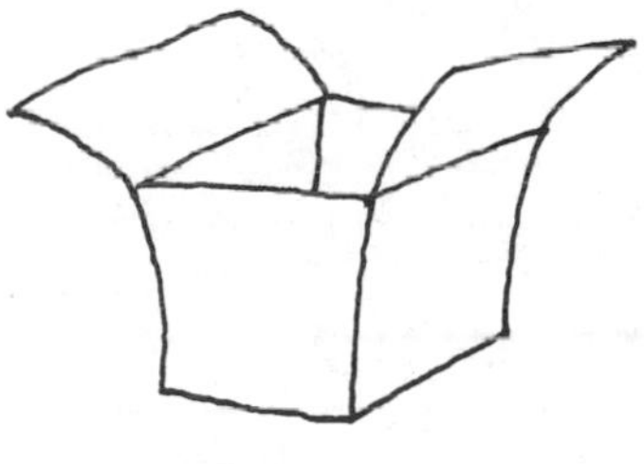

Name ______________________

# Blending Short *u* Words

Blend the letter sounds. Then write the correct word for each picture.

| c | u | t |
|---|---|---|

| c | u | p |
|---|---|---|

| b | u | g |
|---|---|---|

| r | u | g |
|---|---|---|

1. 

2. 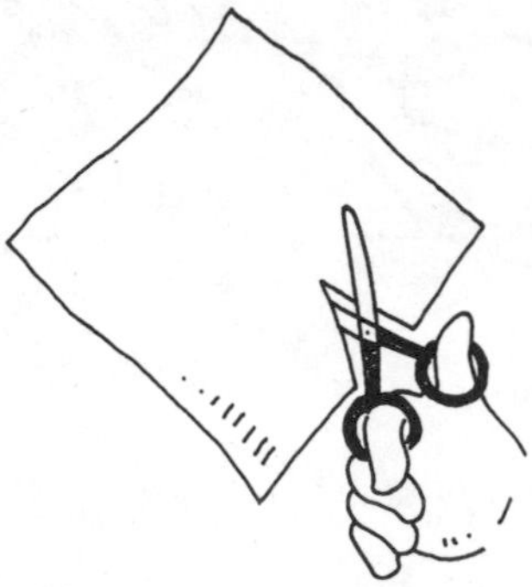

3. 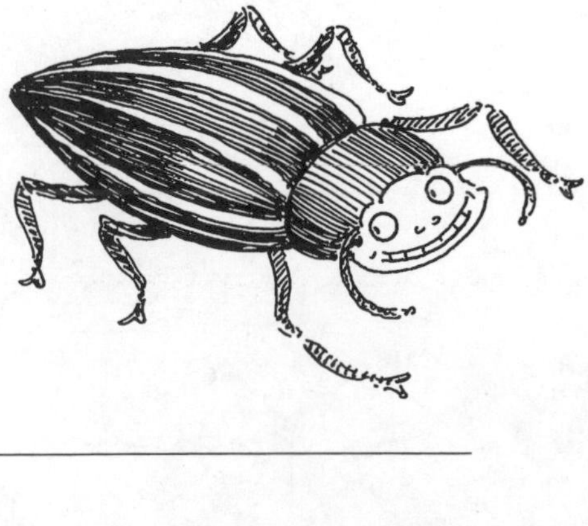

4. 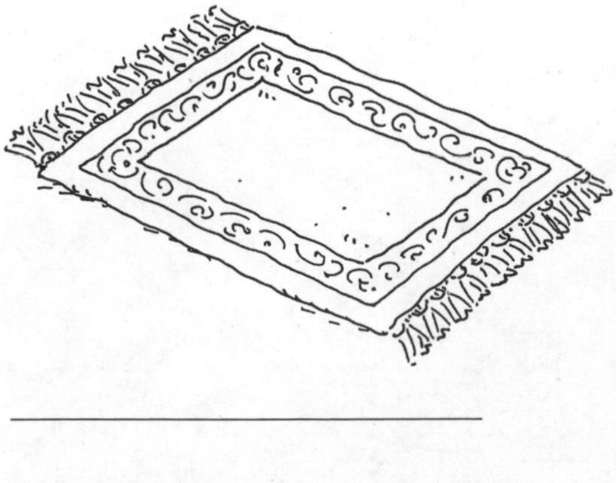

Name ______________________________

# Short *a*, *e*, *i*, *o*, and *u*

Read the words in each box. Draw a line from the correct word to the picture.

| | | | |
|---|---|---|---|
| jet<br>jug | 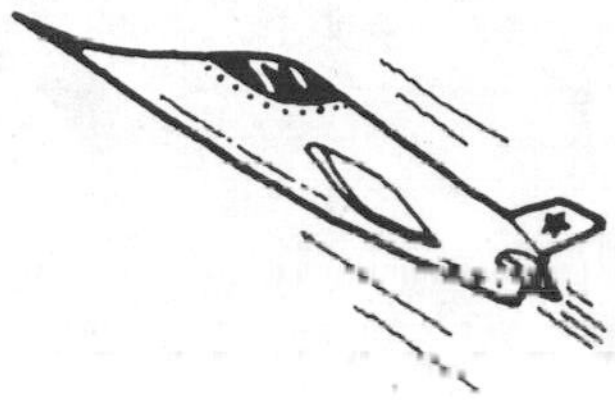 | rug<br>rig |  |
| bug<br>bag |  | mat<br>mug |  |
| nut<br>not |  | hit<br>hut |  |
| hug<br>hog |  | cut<br>cat |  |

Name ______________________

# Begins with *j* or *z*

**Name each picture. Think of the beginning sound. Write j or z.**

j z

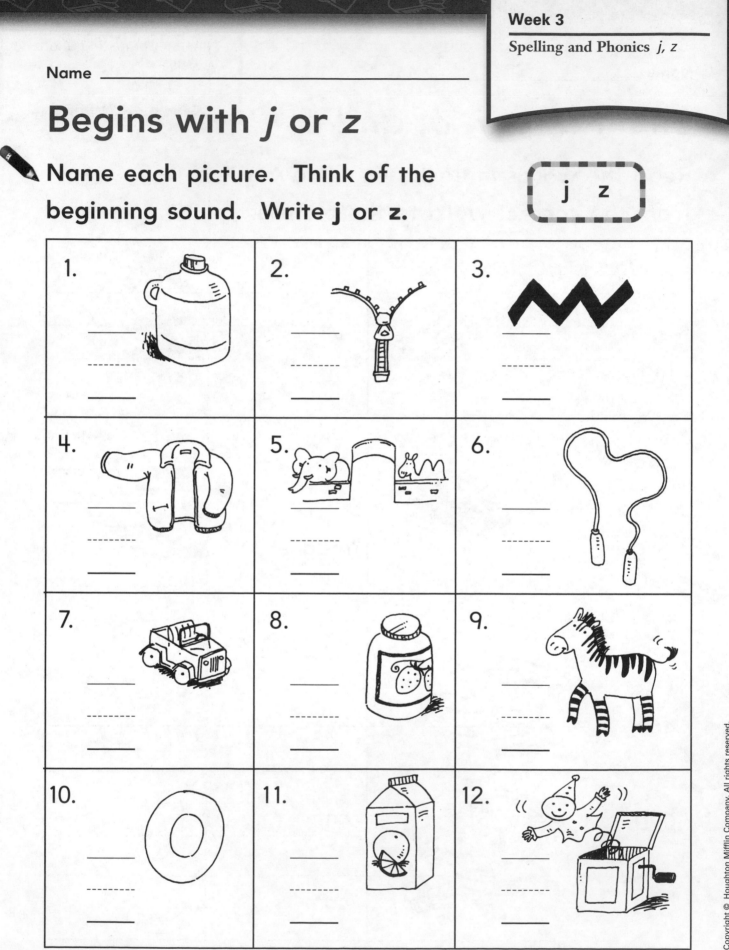

1. 

2. 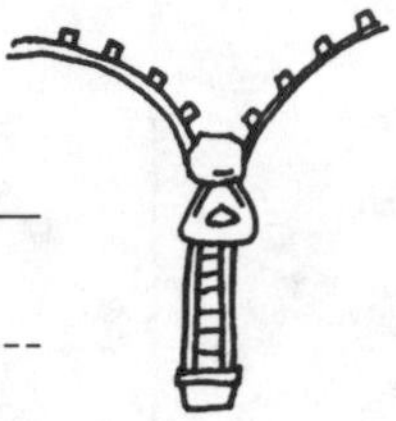

3. 

4. 

5. 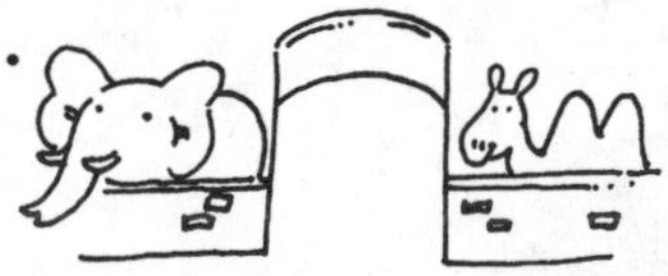

6. 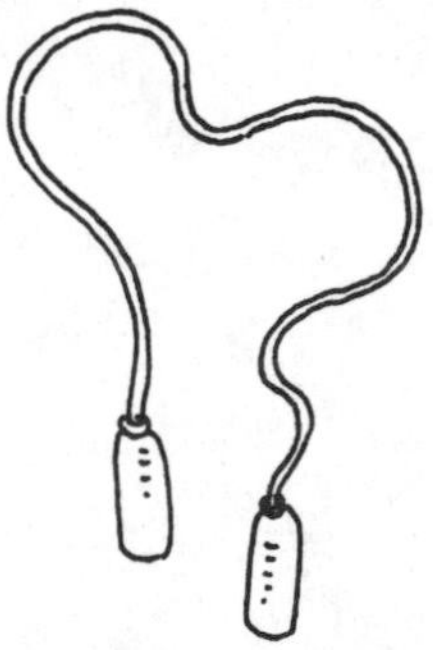

7. 

8. 

9. 

10. 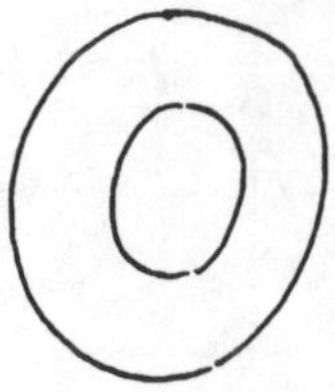

11. 

12. 

Name ______________________________

# Think of the Story

Think about Chapter 2 from the story **What Can a Vet Do?** Answer the questions.

1. Who is in the story?

2. Where do they live?

3. What is the problem?

4. How is the problem solved?

**Week 3**
**High-Frequency Words**

Name ______________________________

# Words to Know

Write a word from the box to complete each sentence in the story.

**Word Bank**

| | | | | | |
|---|---|---|---|---|---|
| does | away | pull | live | are | they |

1. The pet can get __________ .

2. Where __________ the pet go?

3. He can __________ the mat.

4. Can __________ find the pet?

5. They __________ wet.

6. The pet can __________ here!

Name ______________________________

# Words to Know

Cut out and paste each sentence under the picture it matches.

1.

2.

3.

Where are Pat and Dan?

Pat and Dan go away.

Where do Dot and Jan live?

They pull in here.

Does Ken live here?

He does!

Name ______________________________

# Tug Away!

Read the words in the box. Write the correct word to finish each sentence in the play.

**Word Bank**

| | | |
|---|---|---|
| rope | I'm | outside |

Narrator: We are ______________________ .
Get set for the big tug.

Elephant: I have a ____________ .
I am big, and I can tug Hippo.

Hippo: ____________ big, too.
I can tug a lot.
I can get Elephant to quit!

Week 3

Comprehension Check *The Rope Tug*

Name ________________________

# Who Is It?

Circle the name that completes each sentence correctly.

1. ____ can not get in the hut.

   Rat    Elephant    Hippo

2. ____ can get a big rope.

   Hippo    Elephant    Rat

3. Hippo and ____ tug, tug, tug.

   Elephant    Rat    Hippo

4. But they can not pull ____ .

   Hippo    Rat    Elephant

5. Elephant and ____ quit.

   Hippo    Elephant    Rat

6. ____ does a jig.

   Elephant    Hippo    Rat

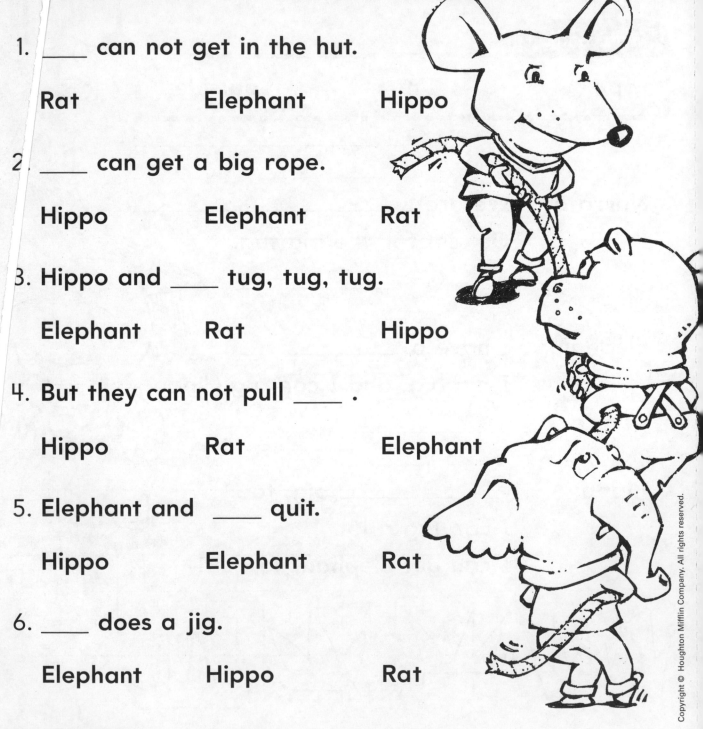

Name ______________________________

# What a Bug!

Draw a picture of a bug.

Write about the bug.

My bug is ______________________________.

It has ______________________________

______________________________.

Name ______________________________

# Double Final Consonants

Read each sentence. Circle the word that ends with a double consonant and write it below.

1. It is fall.

2. Do we have a bass yet?

3. We can add to the can.

4. We have to fill the can!

1. ______________ 2. ______________

3. ______________ 4. ______________

Name ____________________________

# Ending Sounds

Write a word from the box to complete each sentence in the story.

**Word Bank**

sat pack is has bag

Jack has to ______________ .

Can Mack fit in the ______________ ?

Jack ______________ to go.

Mack __________ in the back.

Jack sat. Mack ______________.

They can go!

Name ______________________________

# Words with Short *a*

**Name each picture. Write a if the picture name has the short a sound.**

| | | | |
|---|---|---|---|
| 1.  | 2.  | 3.  | 4.  |
| 5.  | 6.  | 7. 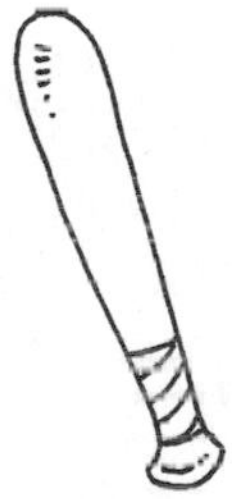 | 8. 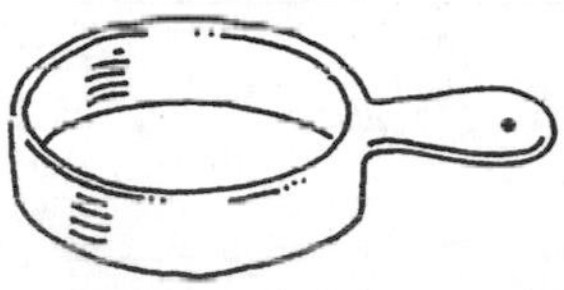 |
| 9. 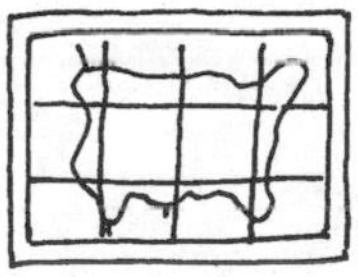 | 10.  | 11.  | 12.  |
| 13. 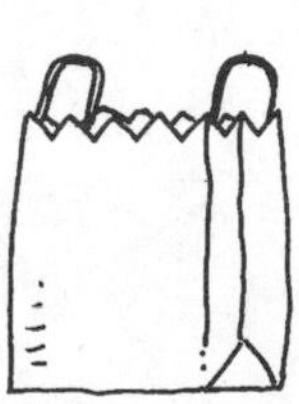 | 14.  | 15.  | 16.  |

Name ____________________

# Words with Short *a*

Read each sentence. Circle the picture of the underlined word. Write the word.

1. What is in the bag?

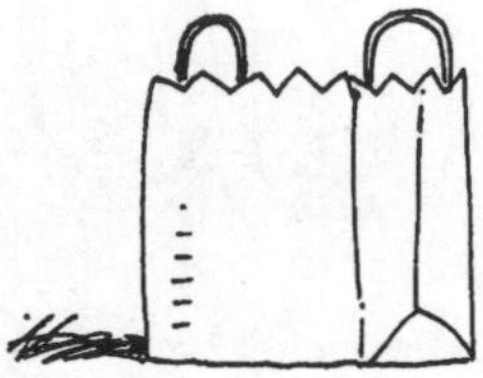

2. We have a yam.

3. We have a ham.

4. We have jam, too.

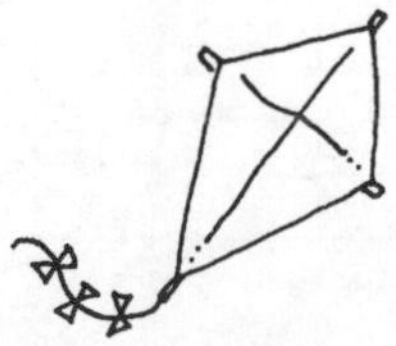
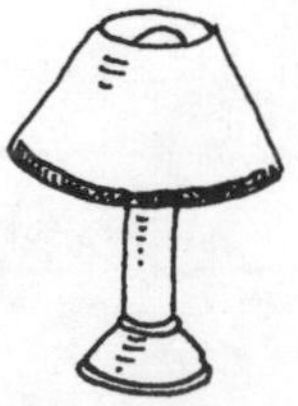

5. Do you have a tack?

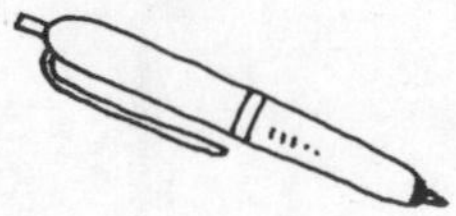

Name ______________________________

# More Than One

**Read each sentence. Circle the picture of the underlined word.**

1. Where are the animals?

2. Ben has cats.

3. Nan has hens.

4. Kit has a pig.

Name ____________________________

# What's It All About?

Read **Big Cats**. Then look at the chart. The topic and main idea are filled in. You add the details.

## Big Cats

What can big cats do?
Big cats can jump.
Big cats can sit, too.
Big cats can live in dens.
Big cats are not pets!

| | |
|---|---|
| Topic | Big cats |
| Main Idea | A big cat can do a lot. |
| Details | |
| | |
| | |
| | |

Name ______________________________

# Words to Know

Write a word from the box to complete each sentence in the story.

**Word Bank**

animal   full   see   flower

## It Is Cold

"Look!" said Zack.

"I __________ a bird."

"Look!" said Jack.

"I see an __________ .

It is __________ of nuts."

"Look!" said Pat.

"I have a fall __________ here."

Name ______________________________

# Words to Know

Look at the picture. Then read each question and circle the answer.

1. Where is the animal?

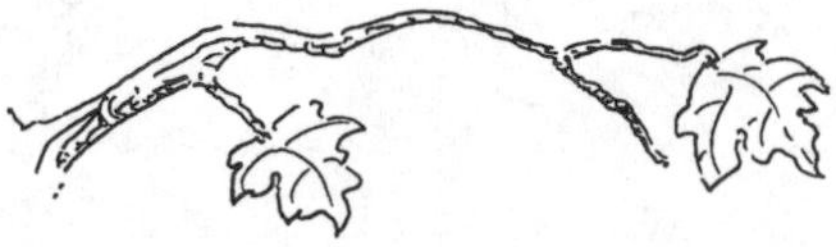

2. Where is the bird?

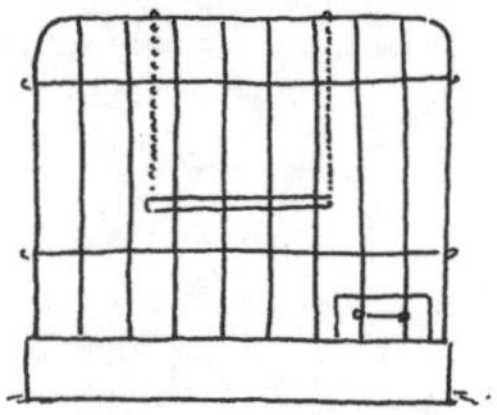

3. What is full of nuts?

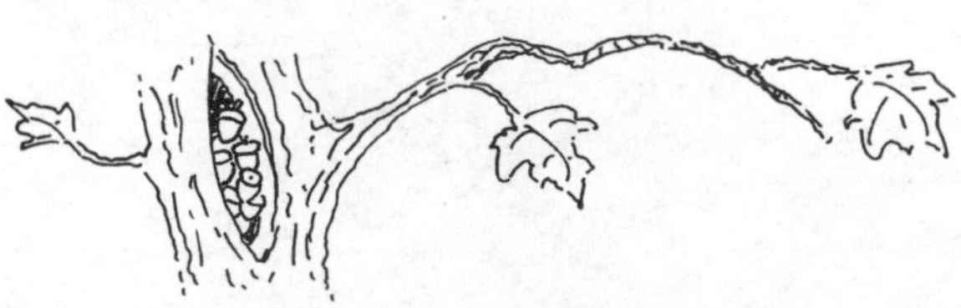
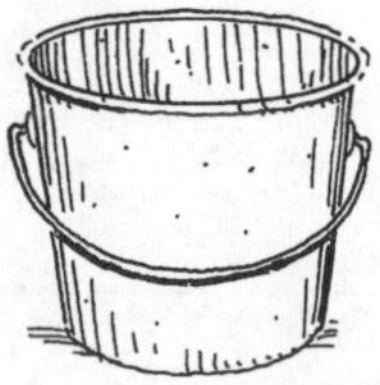

4. Who has the flower?

Name ____________________

# Where We Live . . .

Write a word from the box to complete each sentence in the story.

**Word Bank**

leaves snow summer winter

We live in the South.

It can get cool in the fall.

We jump in the ____________ .

It does not get too cold in the ____________ .

We do not get ____________ .

Spring is not too wet.

We dig in the ____________ .

We can add coal to a "snowman"!

Name ________________________

# Verb Endings *-s, -ed, -ing*

Read each sentence. Circle the sentence that tells about each picture.

1. Nan is looking for Jill to play.

   Ken looks for a bug.

2. Nan kicked the can.

   Nan sees Jill.

3. Nan is going to dig.

   Nan is going to jump.

4. Nan and Jill jumped.

   Nan and Pat filled the box.

Name ________________________________

# Words with Short *i*

**Name each picture. Write i if the picture name has the short i sound.**

| | | | |
|---|---|---|---|
| 1. 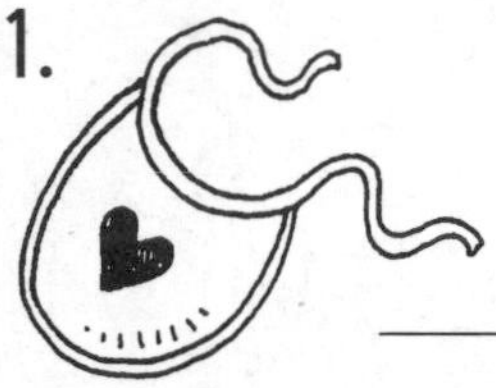 | 2.  | 3.  | 4.  |
| 5.  | 6.  | 7.  | 8.  |
| 9.  | 10.  | 11.  | 12.  |
| 13.  | 14.  | 15.  | 16.  |

Name ______________________________

# Words with Short *i*

Read each sentence, and circle the picture of the underlined word. Write the word.

1. Ben is <u>six</u>.

______________

2. He is looking for a <u>mitt</u>.

______________

3. The <u>wig</u> is not for Ben.

______________

4. The <u>bib</u> fits Em.

______________

5. The cap is for <u>him</u>.

______________

Name ______________________________

# Whose Is It?

**Write the words from the box under the picture they name.**

| |
|---|
| Jill's box |
| Bill's cat |
| Lin's hat |
| Rick's mitt |

1. 

_______________________________

2. 

_______________________________

3. 

_______________________________

4. 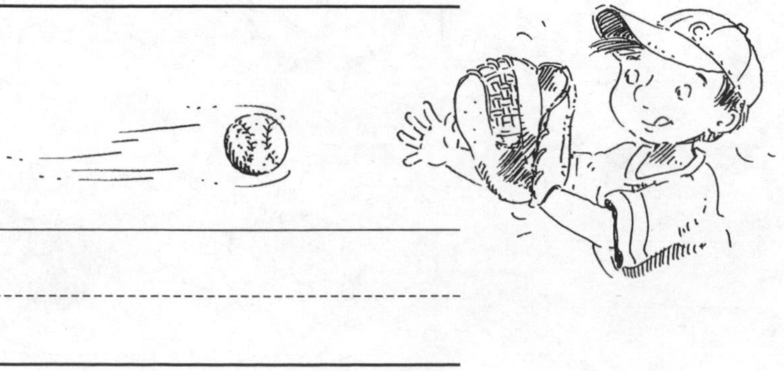

_______________________________

Week 2

Comprehension Making Predictions

Name ______________________________

# What Happens Next?

**Cut out and paste a picture to show what happens next.**

1.

2.

Name ______________________________

# Words to Know

Draw a line from the sentences to the picture they tell about.

1. Bill got the paper first.

2. "Look at the paper, Dad!" said Bill.
   The paper said, "Come eat at Kit's!
   All kids can have a dip and a bit to eat."

3. "Shall I call Kit's?" said Bill.
   "I have never had a dip at Kit's."

4. "Why not?" said Dad.
   "Every kid will go. Get set."

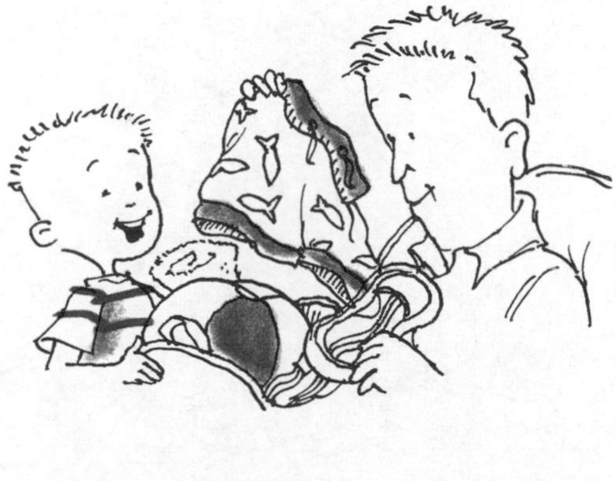

Name ______________________________

# Words to Know

Circle the sentence that tells about each picture.

1.

"Why do we jump?" said Dot Hen.

"Look at the paper first," said Dot Hen.

2.

"Call all the hens to eat," it said.

"I never see all the animals," said Fox.

3.

"Every flower looks tan," said Fox.

"Shall I call Pig to eat, too?" said Dot Hen.

Name ______________________________

# Dinner Time

Write a word from the box to complete each sentence in the story.

**Word Bank**

- trick
- dinner
- dish
- sign

Coyote set up a big sign.

"Eat ______________ at my den,"
it said.

Hen and Pig looked at the ______________ .

"We can go," said Pig.

A sign at the den said, "Sit in the ______________ ."

"It is a ______________ !" said Pig.

"What a bad coyote," said Hen.

Name ______________________________

# What's for Dinner?

Read each question. Circle the correct answer.

1. Who got a paper for a dinner?

   Hen, Fox, Pig, and Coyote got a paper.

   Pig, Hen, and Fox got a paper.

2. Where is the dinner?

   The dinner is at Mr. C's den.

   The dinner is at Pig's hut.

3. Who is Mr. C?

   Mr. C is a big cat.

   Mr. C is a coyote.

4. What did Coyote do to get the animals to sit?

   He said, "It is not a big, bad trick."

   He said, "I will eat one of you."

5. What did the animals have for dinner?

   They had figs and nuts.

   They had yams.

Name ______________________

# The Short *i* Sound

Write a word from the box to complete each sentence in the story.

**Spelling Words**

in
it
him
big
sit
did

1. Dad ________ not see me.

2. ________ filled a box for ________ .

3. The ________ box looked full.

4. I said to Dad, "You can ________ here."

5. Dad said, "What is ________ the box?"

6. I said, "Look in ________ and see!"

Name ______________________

# Naming Parts

Read each sentence, and write the naming part.

1. Tim runs. ____________

2. The cat sits. ____________

3. The pot falls. ____________

4. Dad gets the flowers. ____________

Name ____________________

# Spelling Spree

**Spelling Words**

- in
- it
- him
- big
- sit
- did

Write the missing letter to complete each Spelling Word. Then write the word.

1. d___d ____________
2. h___m ____________
3. ___t ____________

Proofread each sentence. Circle each Spelling Word that is wrong, and write it correctly.

4. The pig is bige. ____________
5. The pig is en a pen! ____________
6. The pig can zit. ____________

Week 2

**Writing** Describing Favorite Foods

Name ______________________________

# Your Favorite Food

**Write sentences to describe your favorite food.**

## What is your favorite food?

______________________________________

______________________________________

## What does it look like?

______________________________________

______________________________________

## How does it taste?

______________________________________

______________________________________

Name ______________________________

# Clusters with *r*

Name each picture. Circle the letters that stand for the beginning sounds.

| | | | |
|---|---|---|---|
| 1.  cr pr fr | 2.  fr br tr | 3.  br gr tr | 4.  pr gr tr |
| 5.  br cr tr | 6.  br dr fr | 7.  br gr tr | 8.  cr dr tr |
| 9.  cr fr pr | 10.  cr pr fr | 11.  br dr pr | 12.  br fr pr |
| 13.  br fr pr | 14. 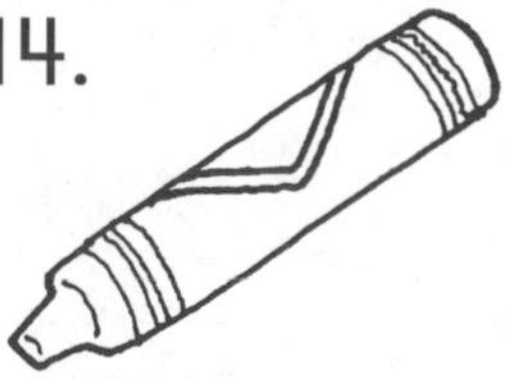 cr pr fr | 15.  dr fr pr | 16.  tr fr dr |

Name ______________________________

# Clusters with *r*

**Circle the word that names each picture.**

**Write the word.**

1. 

**brick** **brim**

2. 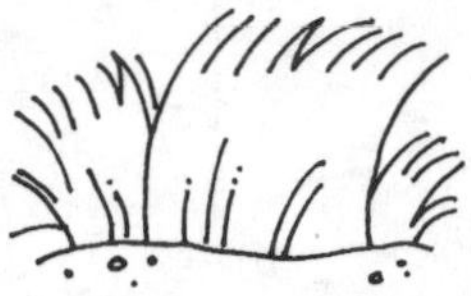

**grab** **grass**

3. 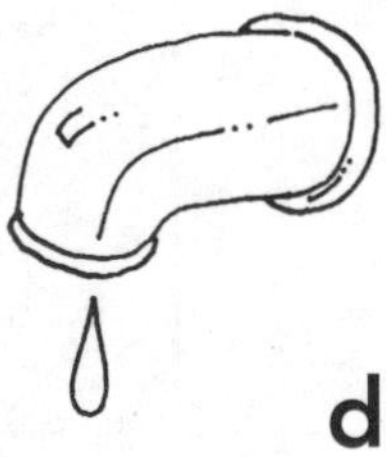

**drag** **drip**

4. 

**crib** **crab**

5. 

**trap** **trip**

6. 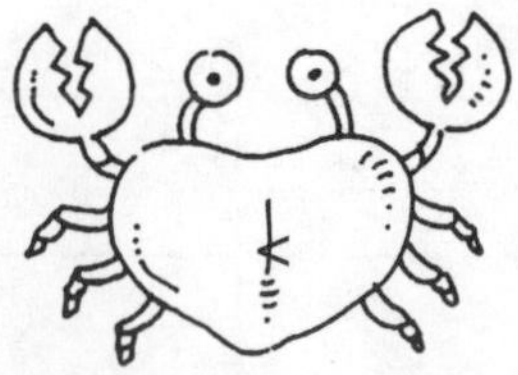

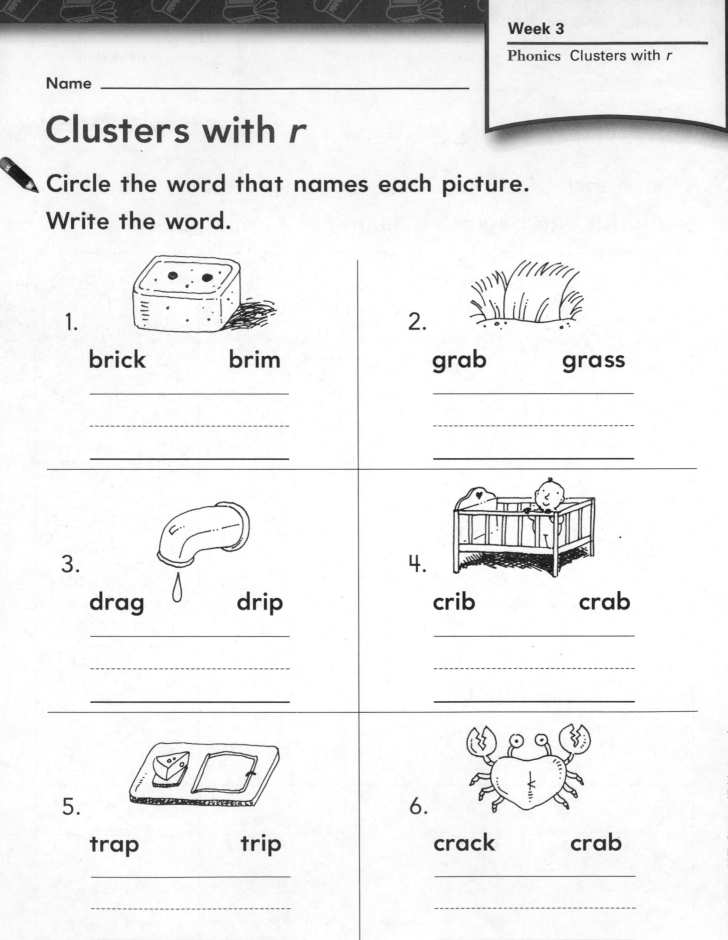

**crack** **crab**

Name ______________________

# Contractions with 's

Rewrite each sentence. Use a word from the box in place of the underlined words.

**Word Bank**

| He's | It's | What's | Where's | Who's |
|---|---|---|---|---|

1. Who is calling you?

2. He is my dad.

3. Where is my hat?

4. What is in the box?

5. It is Dad's hat!

Name ______________________________

# Which Is Which?

Use the words in the box to list words under **Can Eat** or **Can Not Eat**.

**Word Bank**

| | | | |
|---|---|---|---|
| ham | crab | brick | jam |
| fox | map | ribs | hill |

| Can Eat | Can Not Eat |
|---|---|
| ______________ | ______________ |
| ______________ | ______________ |
| ______________ | ______________ |
| ______________ | ______________ |

Name ____________________

# Words to Know

Read the story. Color the picture that matches the story.

"Look!" said Kris. "I see many animals!"
"Me, too!" said Brad.
Kris said, "I see some green and brown frogs!"
"Me, too!" said Brad.
Kris said, "And I also see a bird as blue as my cap!"
"Me, too," said Brad.
"I like to look at the colors of all the pets," said Kris.
"Me, too!" said the bird.
"Funny bird!" said Brad.

Name ______________________

# Words to Know

**Read the words in the box. Write the words that name colors on the fish. Write the other words on the boat.**

**Word Bank**

- also
- blue
- brown
- color
- funny
- green
- like
- many
- some

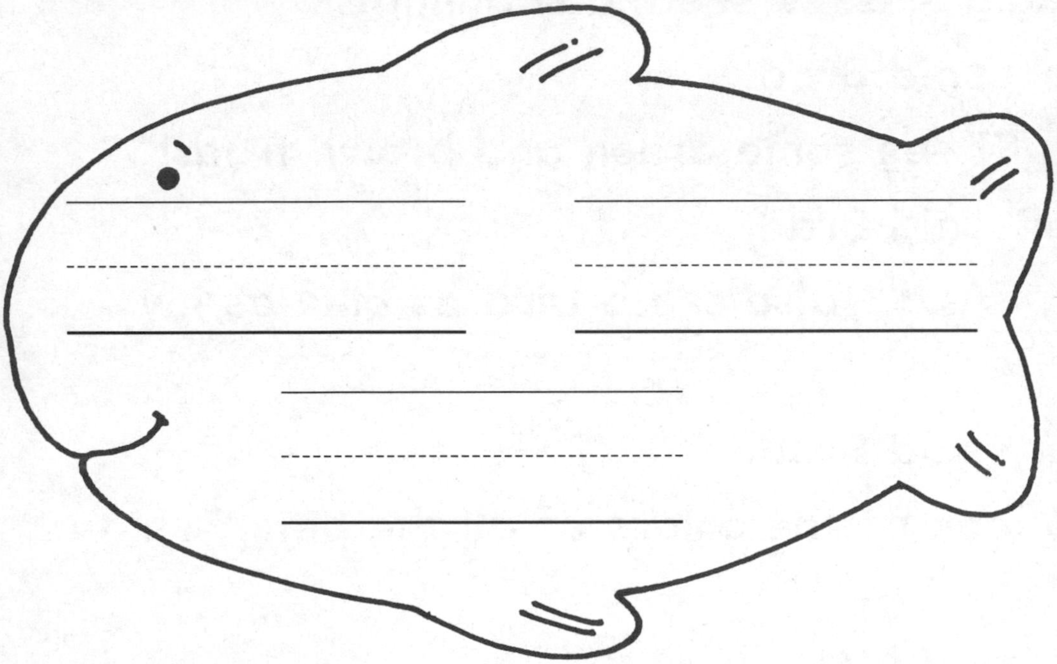

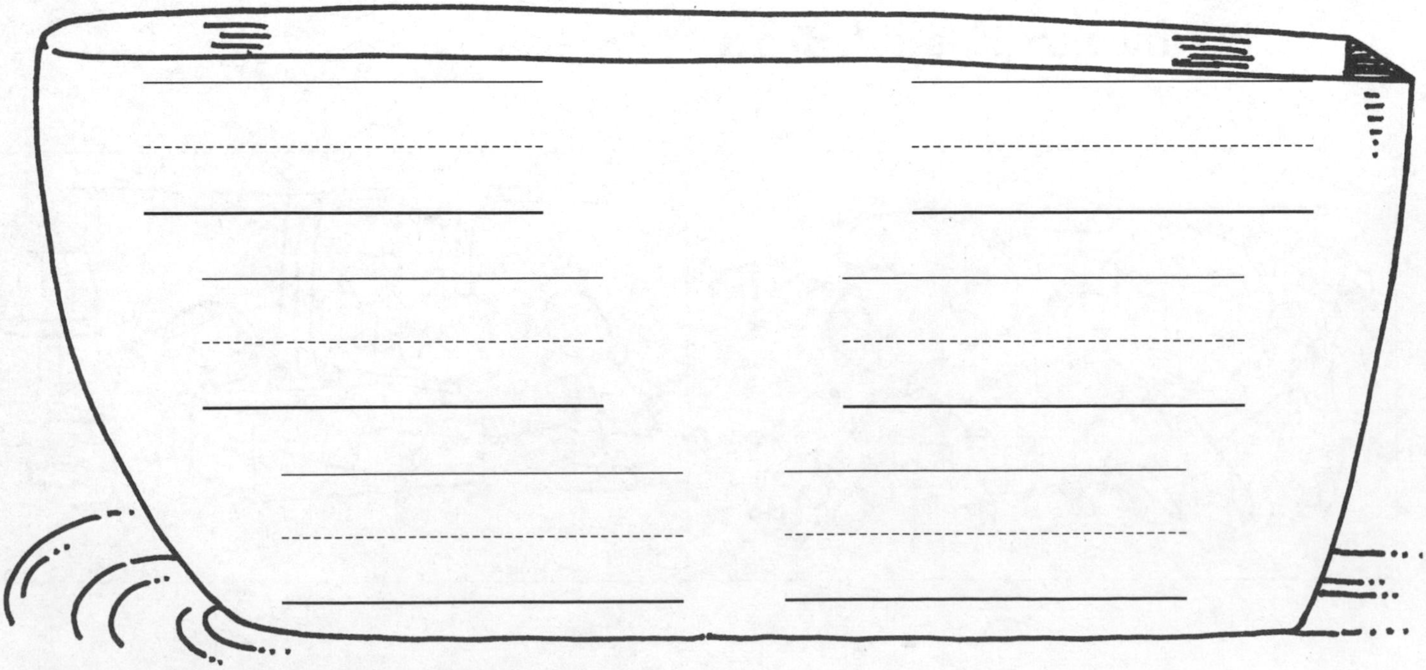

Name ______________________________

# Words to Know

Write a word from the box to complete each sentence. Use the pictures to help you.

**Word Bank**

change
fish
sea
whales

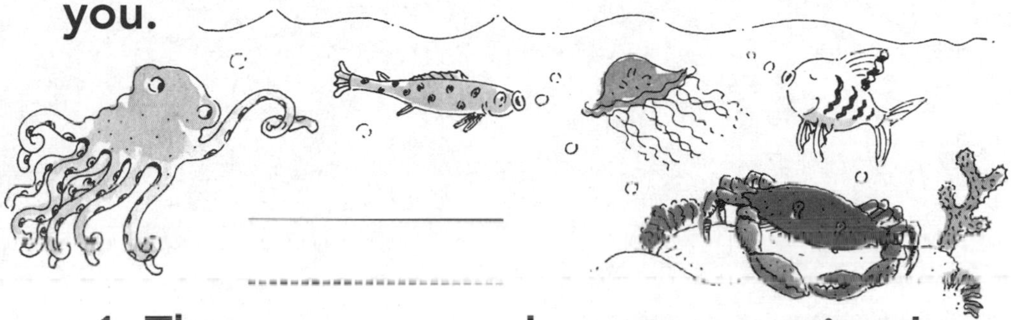

1. The __________ has many animals.

2. Some __________ like to eat krill.

3. This __________ lives in the sea, too.

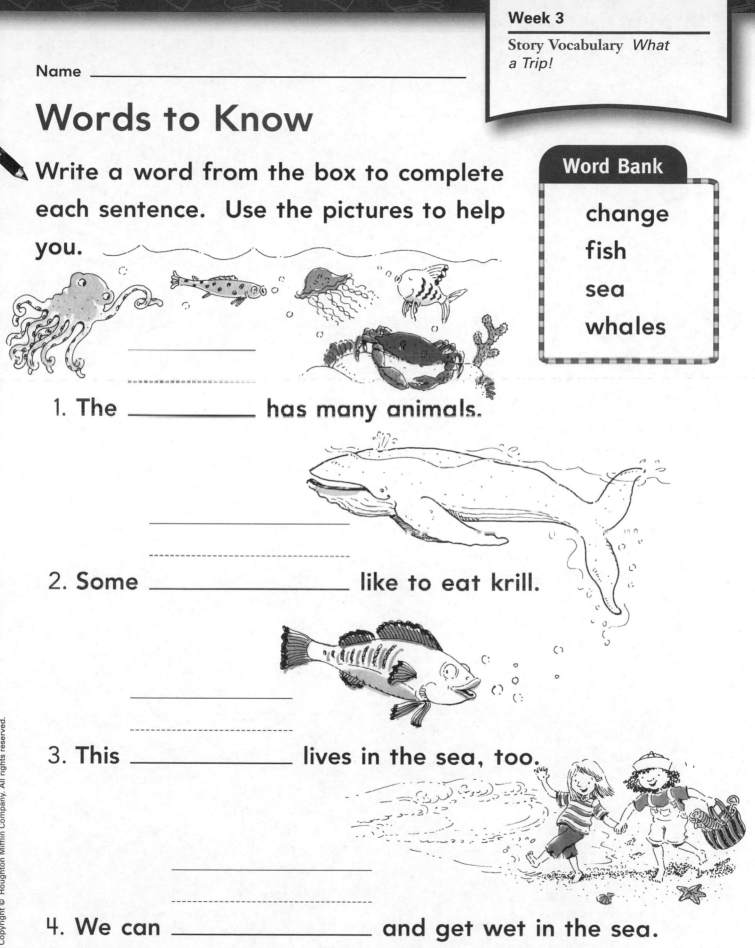

4. We can __________ and get wet in the sea.

Name ______________________________

# What Did You See?

Read each question. Cut out and paste the correct answer under the question.

1. Where's the funny fish?

2. What can grab?

3. What can zig and zag?

A crab can.

Here it is!

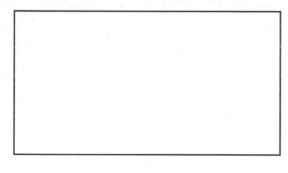

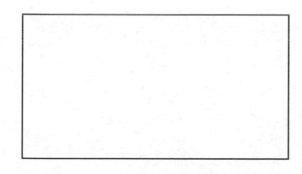

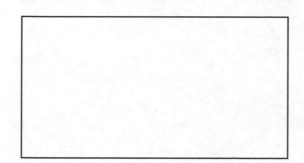

Some fish can zig and zag.

Name ________________________

# Clusters with *r*

Write a word from the box to complete each sentence in the story.

**Word Bank**

trip crab drip grin grab trap

1. Dan will go on a ____________ .

2. He will ____________ his bags.

3. Look at Dad ____________ !

4. Dad and Dan set the ____________ .

5. Dad has a big ____________ .

6. Dan said, "Do not let it ____________ on me!"

Name ______________________

# Make Them Complete!

**Write an action part from the box to complete each sentence in the story.**

| | | | |
|---|---|---|---|
| gets a bass | jump | eat | fix the fish |

1. Some fish ______________________ .

2. Mom ______________________ .

3. Dad and the kids ______________________ .

4. Then they ______________________ !

Name ______________________

# Spelling Spree

**Spelling Words**
- trip
- crab
- drip
- grin
- grab
- trap

Add the missing letter to write each Spelling Word.

1. t __ ap = ____________
2. d __ ip = ____________
3. g __ ab = ____________

Proofread each sentence. Circle each Spelling Word that is wrong, and write it correctly.

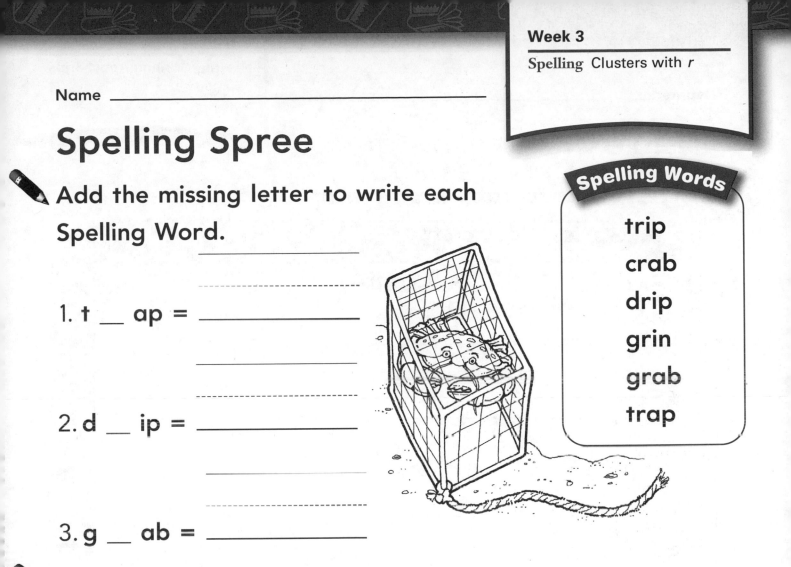

4. We go on a tirp. ____________
5. We get a krab! ____________
6. We grinn. ____________

Name ______________________________

# Plan Your Trip!

Write your ideas about your trip.

Where will you go?

______________________________

______________________________

How will you get there?

______________________________

______________________________

What will you do there?

______________________________

______________________________

How will you get home?

______________________________

______________________________

Name ______________________

# Spelling Review

Each Spelling Word is missing one letter. Write the missing letter.

**Spelling Words**

drip big trap an grab crab

The missing letter is the first sound you hear

in .

1. ___n

The missing letter is the first sound you hear

in .

2. b___g

Write two letters to complete each Spelling Word.

3. ______ab
4. ______ap
5. ______ab
6. ______ip

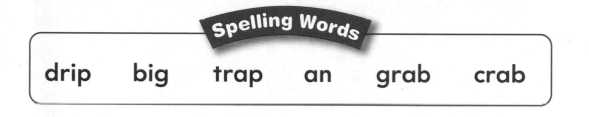

Name ______________________

# Spelling Spree

Write a Spelling Word in each blank.

**Spelling Words**

at had in it big drip

1. It can ____________.

2. The cat hid ______ a bag.

3. I __________ a bad cold.

Proofread each sentence. Circle each Spelling Word that is wrong, and write it correctly.

4. I am on a bigg trip! __________

5. I look att a crab. __________

6. Et can grab. __________

Name ______________________________

# Clusters with *l*

**Name each picture. Circle the letters that stand for the beginning sounds.**

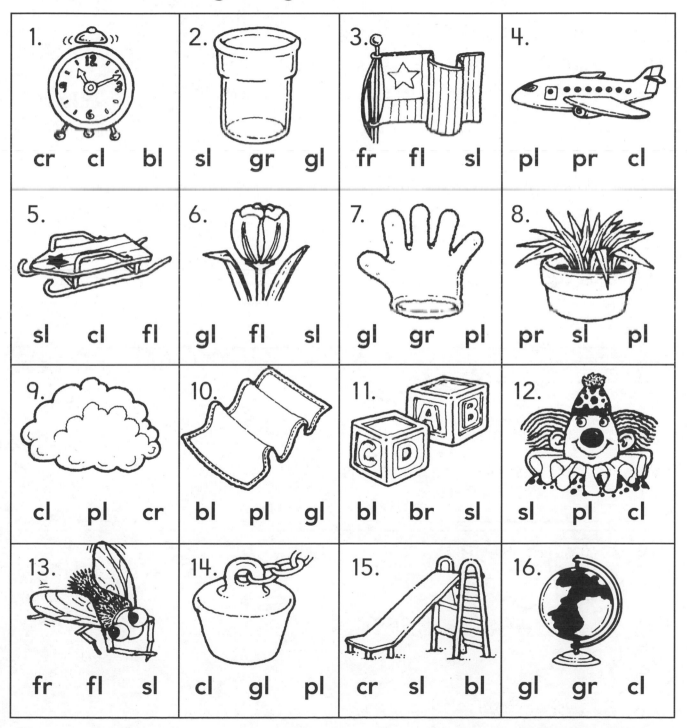

| | | | |
|---|---|---|---|
| 1.  cr cl bl | 2. 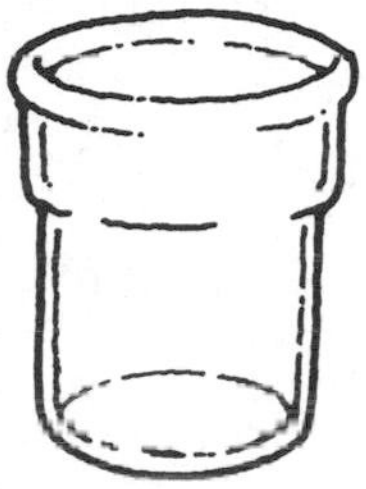 sl gr gl | 3.  fr fl sl | 4. 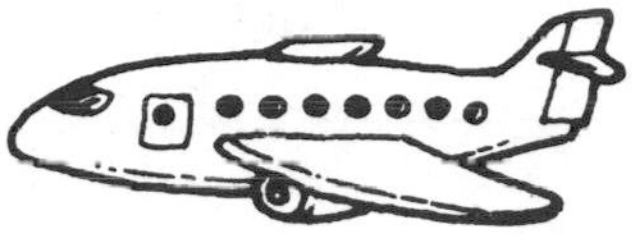 pl pr cl |
| 5. 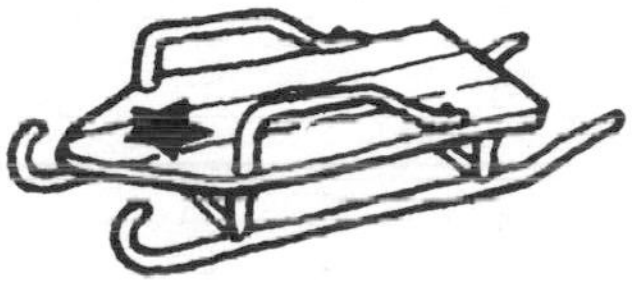 sl cl fl | 6.  gl fl sl | 7.  gl gr pl | 8.  pr sl pl |
| 9.  cl pl cr | 10. 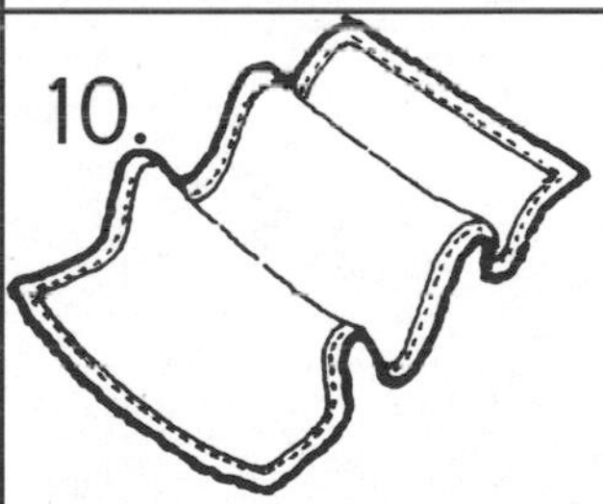 bl pl gl | 11.   bl br sl | 12.  sl pl cl |
| 13.  fr fl sl | 14.  cl gl pl | 15.  cr sl bl | 16.  gl gr cl |

Name ______________________

# Clusters with *l*

**Circle the word that names each picture.**
**Write the word.**

1. 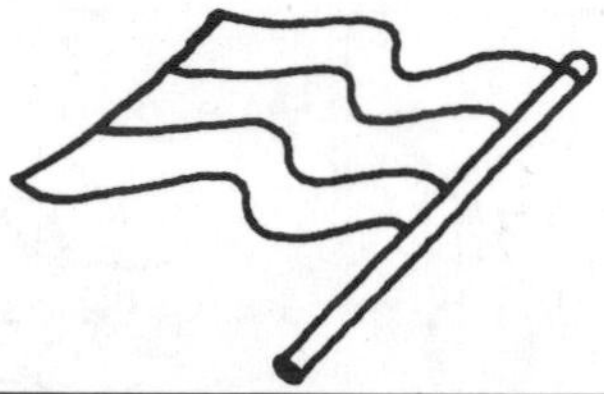
flat
flag

2. 
clock
class

3. 
glass
grass

4. 
block
blot

5. 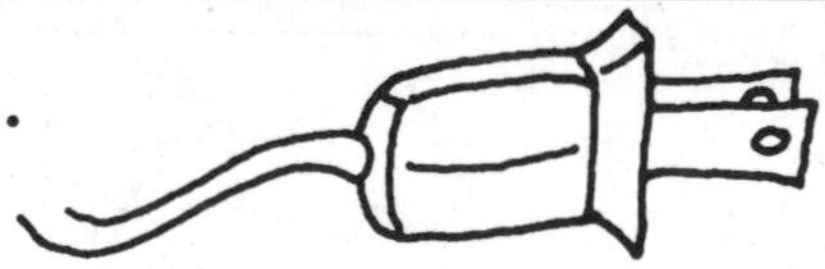
plug
slug

6. 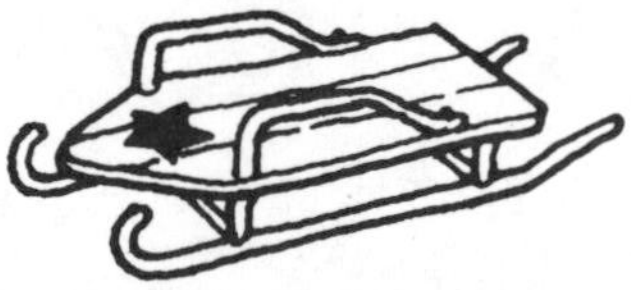
sled
slacks

7. 
flap
clap

8. 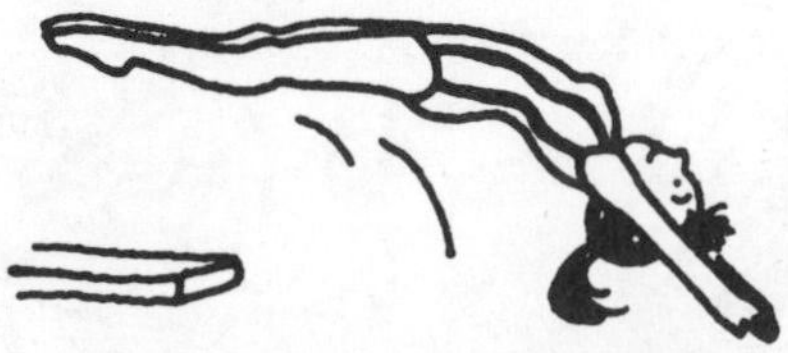
flat
flip

Name ______________________

# Words with Short *o*

**Name each picture. Write o if the picture name has the short o sound.**

1. 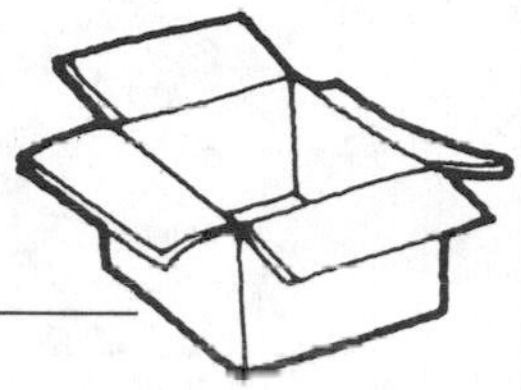 ___

2. 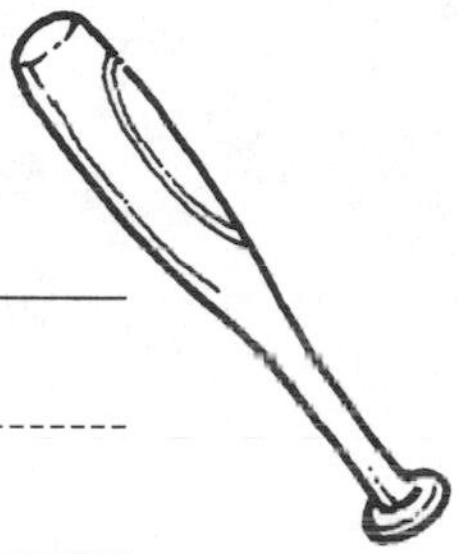 ___

3.  ___

4. 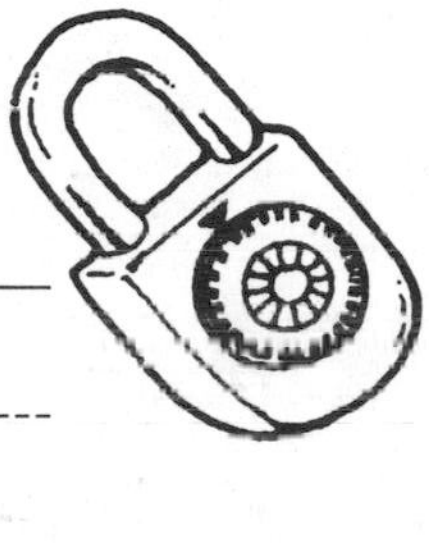 ___

5.  ___

6. 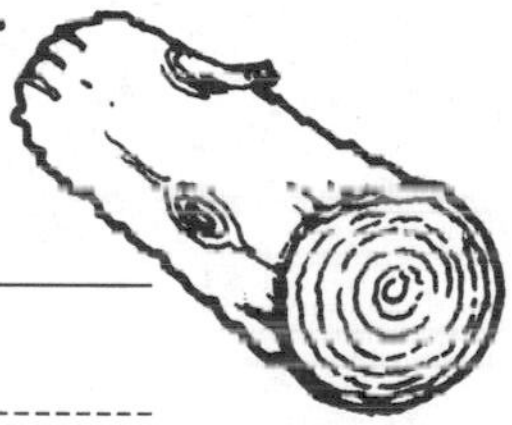 ___

7. 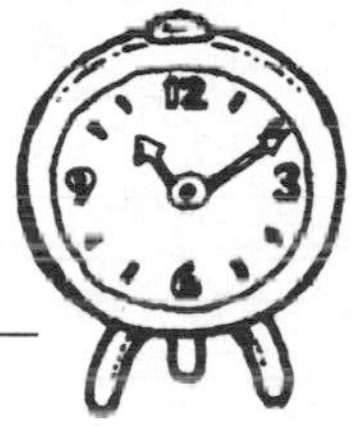 ___


8.  ___

9.  ___


10. 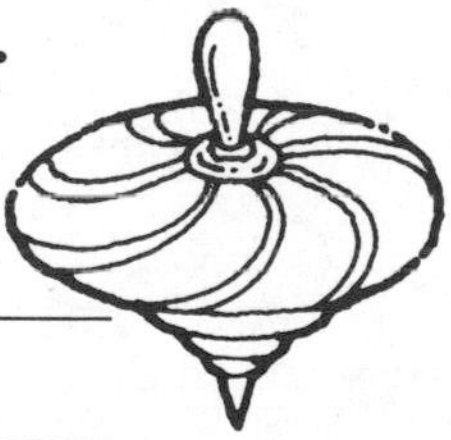 ___

11. 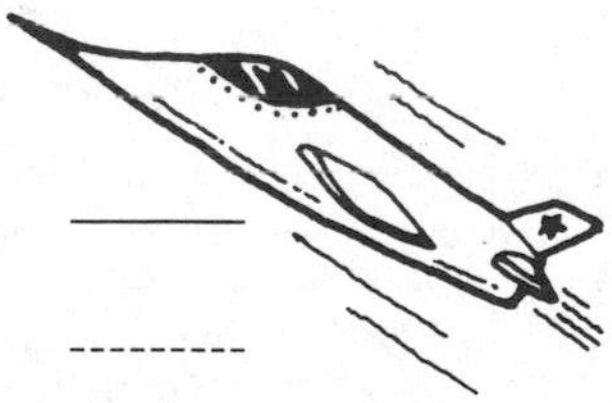 ___

12. 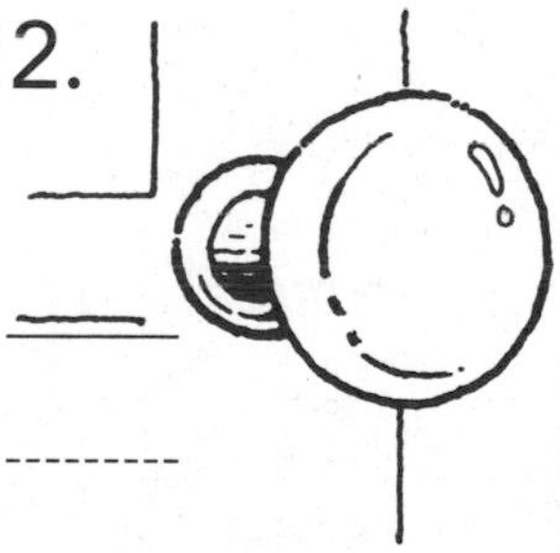 ___

13. 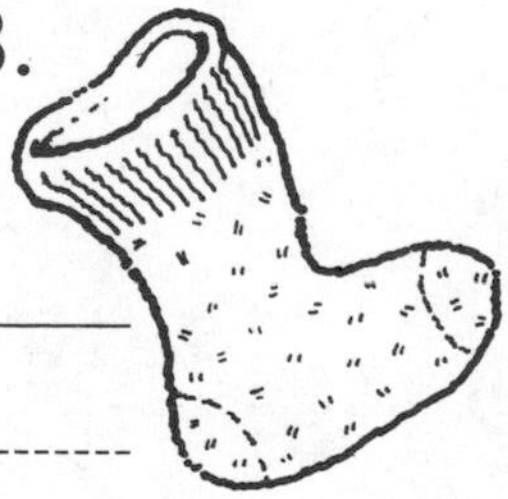 ___

14.  ___

15.  ___

16.  ___

Name ______________________________

# Words with Short *o*

Read each sentence, and circle the picture of the underlined word. Write the word.

1. Dot can pack for a trip.

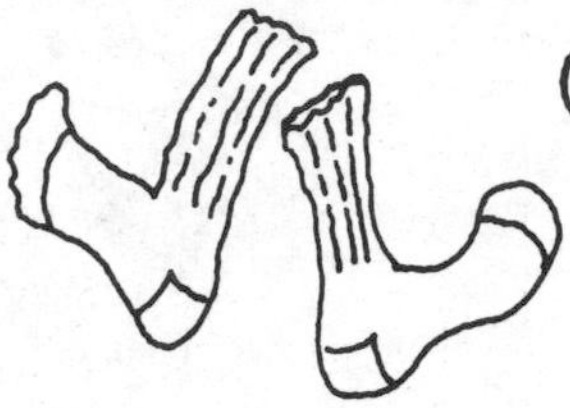

2. Bob sees a clock.

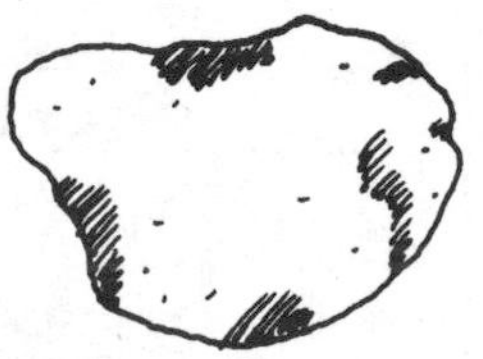

3. See Dot's doll.

4. See Dot's socks.

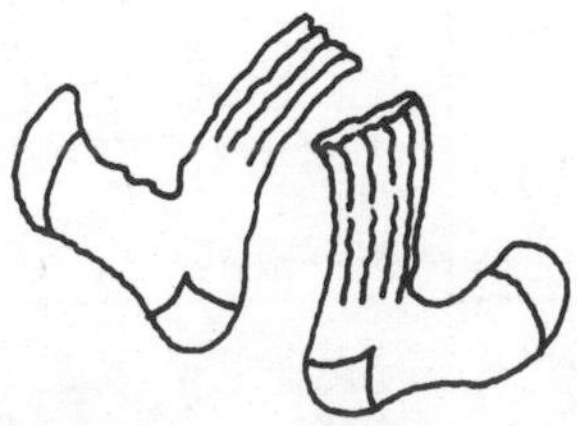

5. See Dot's blocks.

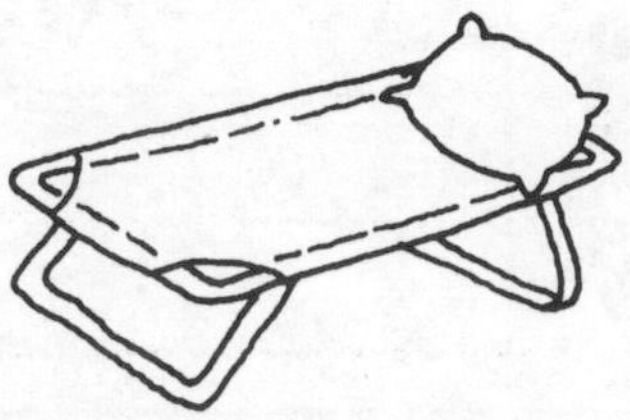

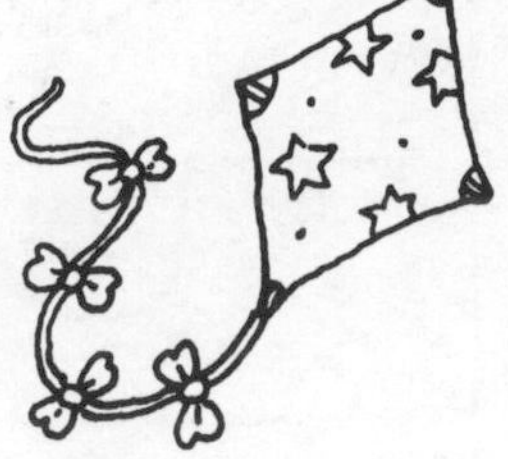

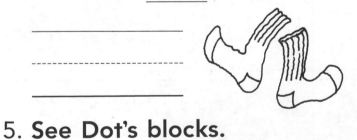

Name ____________________



# Drawing Conclusions

Read the sentences. Write your conclusion.

1. Dan is cold.
   Dan sees a hat.

   ____________________

   Dan will ____________________

   ____________________

2. The vet looks at the pet.
   The pet is not sick.

   ____________________

   The pet will ____________________

   ____________________

Name ______________________________

# Words to Know

Write a word from the box to complete each sentence in the story.

**Word Bank**

your  love  picture  children

Come see the people in my family.

Here is a ____________________.

We have a mother, a father, and two

____________________.

We get lots of ____________________.

Who's in ____________________family?

Name ______________________________

# Words to Know

Cut out the pictures. Paste each picture above the sentence that goes with it.

1. "Come here and see my pictures," said Jan.

2. Here is a picture of six people.

3. See the mother and father hug the children.

4. I love the picture of your family.

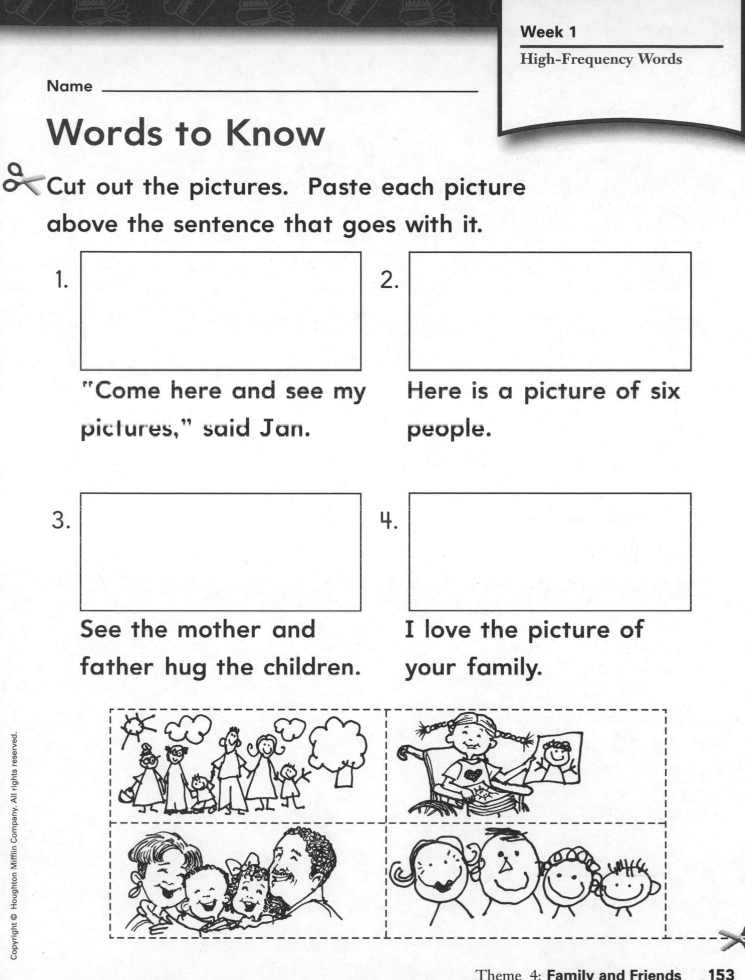

Name ____________________

# Family Fun

Write a word from the box to complete each sentence.

**Word Bank**

ball garden picnic snap

1. Some families like to pick food in a ____________.

2. Some families like to have a ____________.

3. Some families like to kick a ____________.

4. Some families also like to ____________ pictures.

Name ____________________

# Families

Circle the word that completes each sentence.
Write the word in the sentence.

1. A family can have ____________.

and children go

2. Families can get lots of ____________.

jump love four

3. Some families have ____________.

pets eat fall

4. Some families like to ____________.

cold food jog

Name ____________________

# The Short *o* Sound

Write a word to complete each sentence.

**Spelling Words**

on not got box hot top

1. It is ____________.
2. Tom ____________ a big box.
3. See what he did to the ____________!
4. The box is ____________ Bob.
5. It is on ____________ of Bob.
6. It's ____________ hot in the box.

Name ______________________

# Make It a Sentence!

Write a naming part to complete each sentence.

| | |
|---|---|
| The cat | Kim |

1. ______________ likes to kick and pass.

2. ______________ likes to eat catnip.

Write an action part to complete each sentence.

| | |
|---|---|
| lives in a den | gets a job |

3. Dad ______________________.

4. The fox ______________________.

Name ____________________

# Spelling Spree

Write the missing letter. Write the word.

**Spelling Words**

on not got box hot top

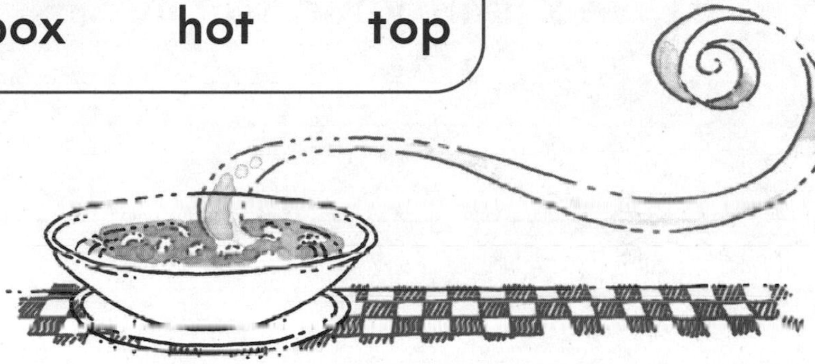

1. h ___ t ____________

2. g ___ t ____________

3. n ___ t ____________

Proofread each sentence. Circle each Spelling Word that is wrong, and write it correctly.

4. I have a big bocks. ____________

5. Fran and I sit un it. ____________

6. The tp falls in! ____________

Name ______________________________

# What Is Your Answer?

Write a complete sentence to answer each question.

1. Who is in your family?

______________________________

______________________________

______________________________

2. What fun does your family have?

______________________________

______________________________

______________________________

Name ________________________________

# Clusters with *s*

**Name each picture. Circle the letters that stand for the beginning sounds.**

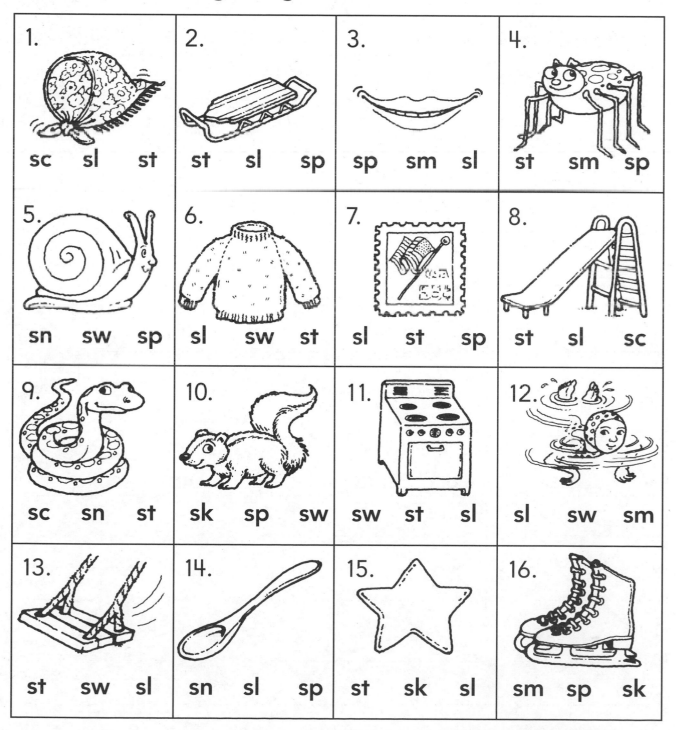

| | | | |
|---|---|---|---|
| 1.  sc sl st | 2.  st sl sp | 3. 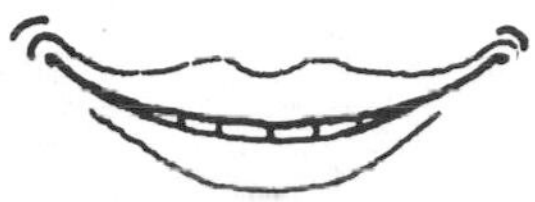 sp sm sl | 4.  st sm sp |
| 5.  sn sw sp | 6.  sl sw st | 7.  sl st sp | 8. 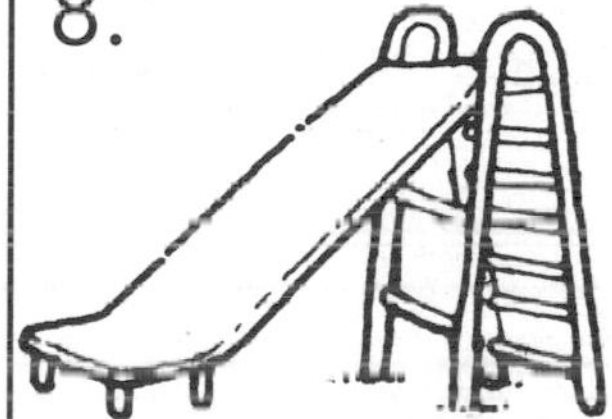 st sl sc |
| 9.  sc sn st | 10.  sk sp sw | 11. 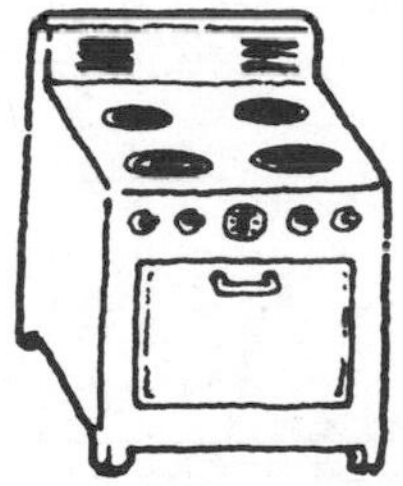 sw st sl | 12.  sl sw sm |
| 13. 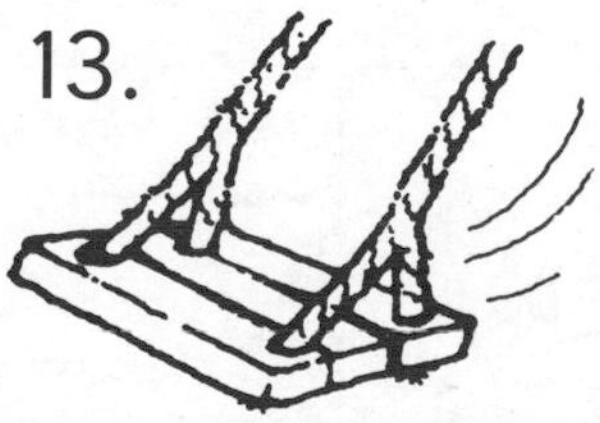 st sw sl | 14. 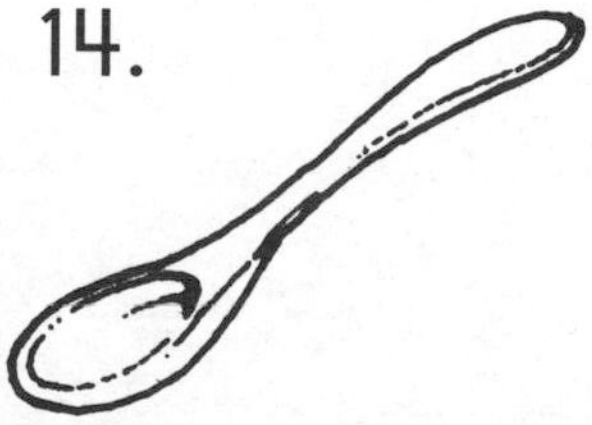 sn sl sp | 15. 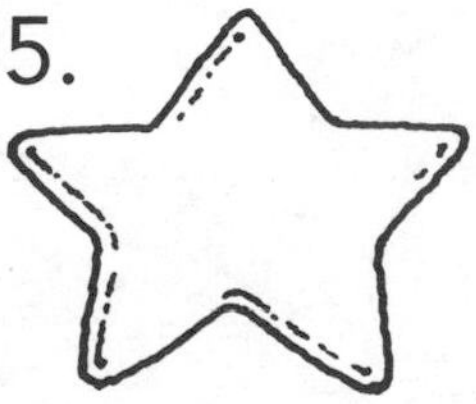 st sk sl | 16.  sm sp sk |

Name ______________________________

# Clusters with *s*

**Read each word. Write s before each word. Read the new word.**

| | | |
|---|---|---|
| 1. ____led | 2. ____tick | 3. ____nap |
| 4. ____cat | 5. ____pin | 6. ____top |
| 7. ____pot | 8. ____kid | 9. ____lip |
| 10. ____mock | 11. ____well | 12. ____tack |

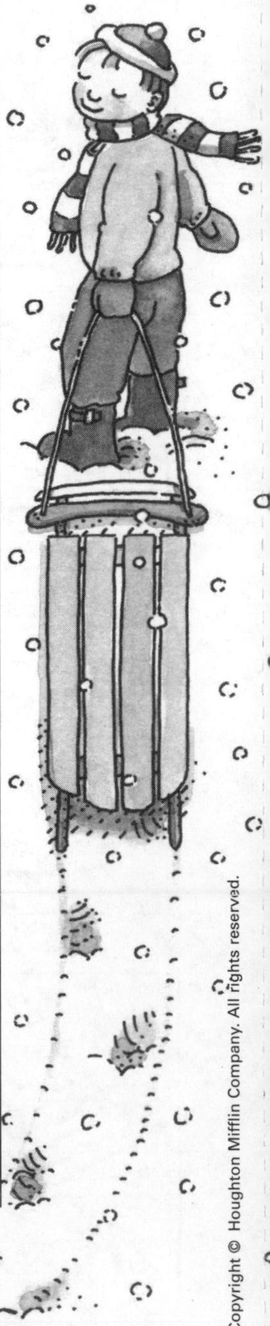

Name ______________________________

# Words with Short *e*

Name each picture. Write e if the picture name has the short e sound.

| | | | |
|---|---|---|---|
| 1.  | 2.  | 3.  | 4.  |
| 5. 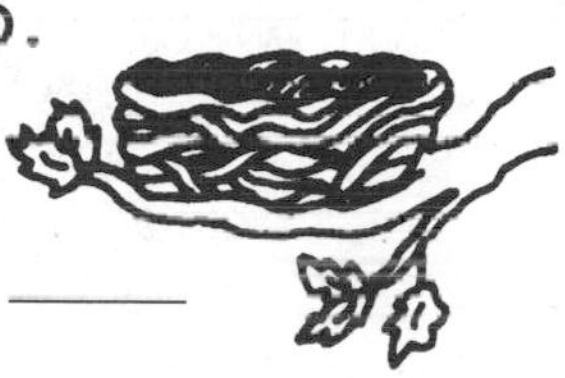 | 6.  | 7.  | 8.  |
| 9. 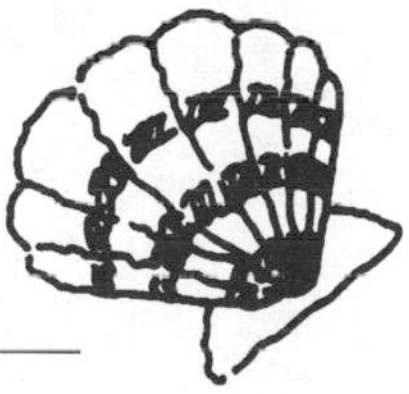 | 10.  | 11. 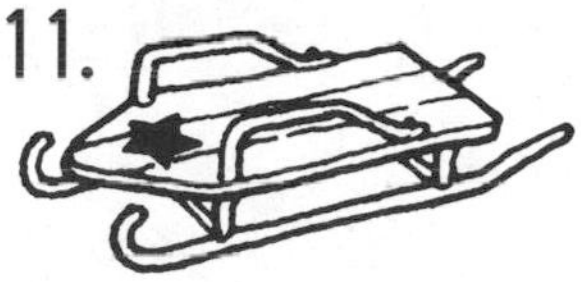 | 12.  |
| 13.  | 14.  | 15.  | 16.  |

Name ______________________

# Words with Short *e*

Read each sentence. Circle the picture of the underlined word. Write the word.

1. The bird has a <u>nest</u>.

2. The pig has a <u>pen</u>.

3. The bug has a <u>web</u>.

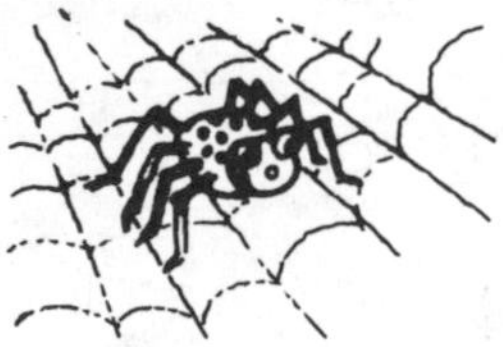

4. The cub has a <u>den</u>.

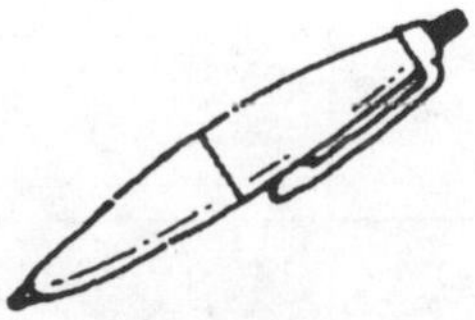

5. Pat has a <u>bed</u>.

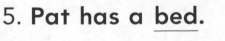

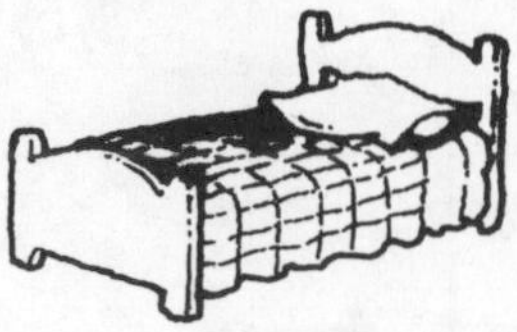
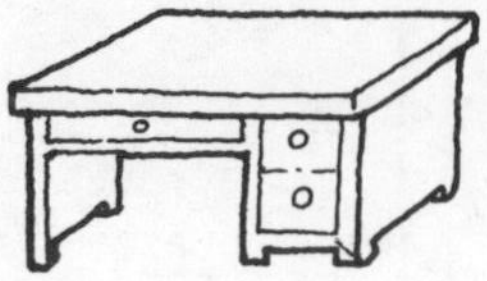

Name ______________________________

# Silent *kn*, *wr*, *gn*

Name each picture. Circle the pair of letters that begin each picture name. Write the two letters.

1. 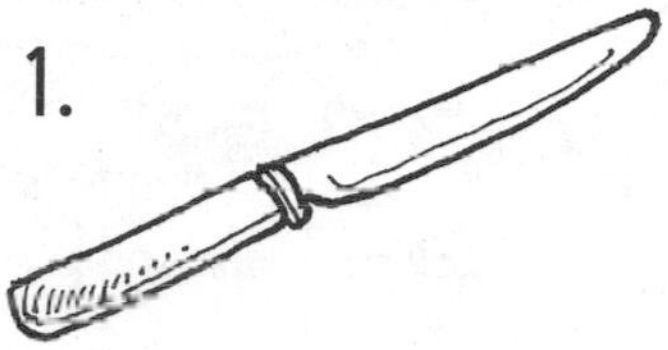
wr kn

2. 
wr kn

3. 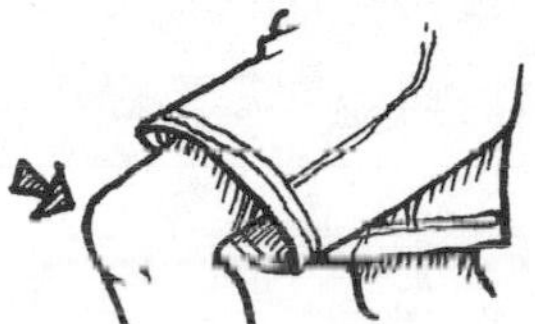
wr kn

4. 
wr kn

5. 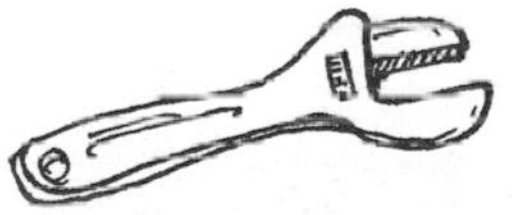
gn wr

6. 
gn wr

7. 
wr gn

8. 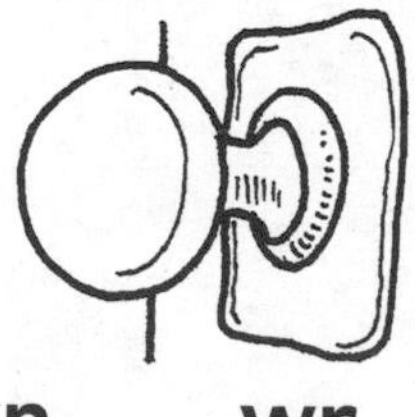
kn wr

9. 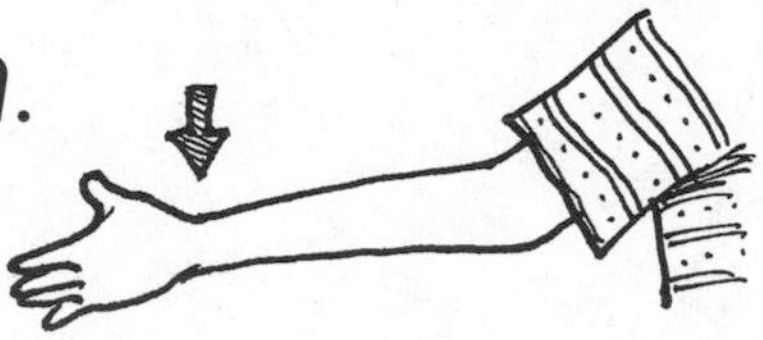
kn wr

Name ______________________________

# Alike and Different

**Think about what a girl and a dog can do. Read each phrase in the box. Write it in the chart where it belongs.**

| | | |
|---|---|---|
| can not spell | can pick flowers | can eat |
| can jump | can not pick flowers | can spell |

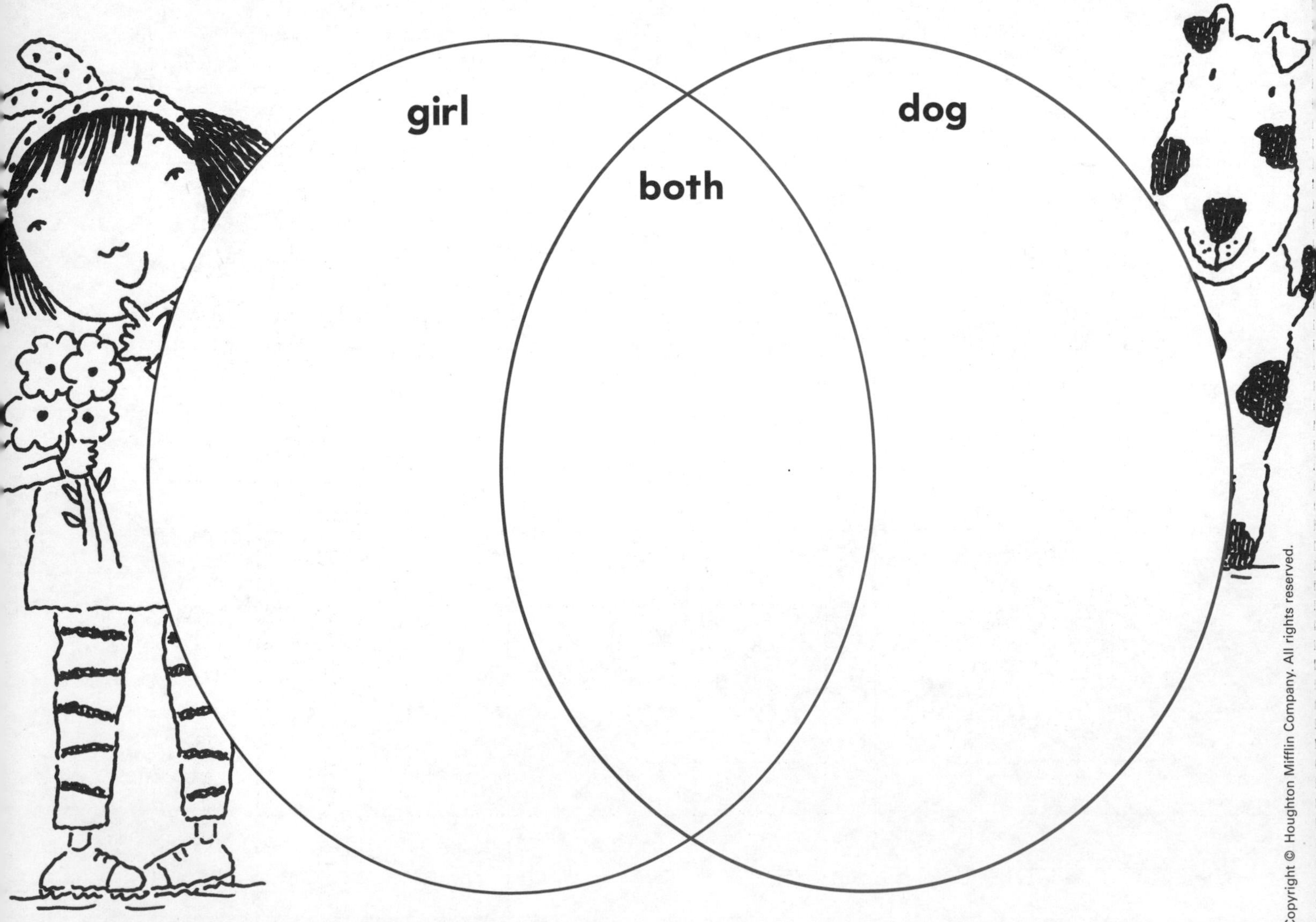

Name ____________________

# Words to Know

Cut out and paste each sentence next to the picture it describes.

1.

2.

3.

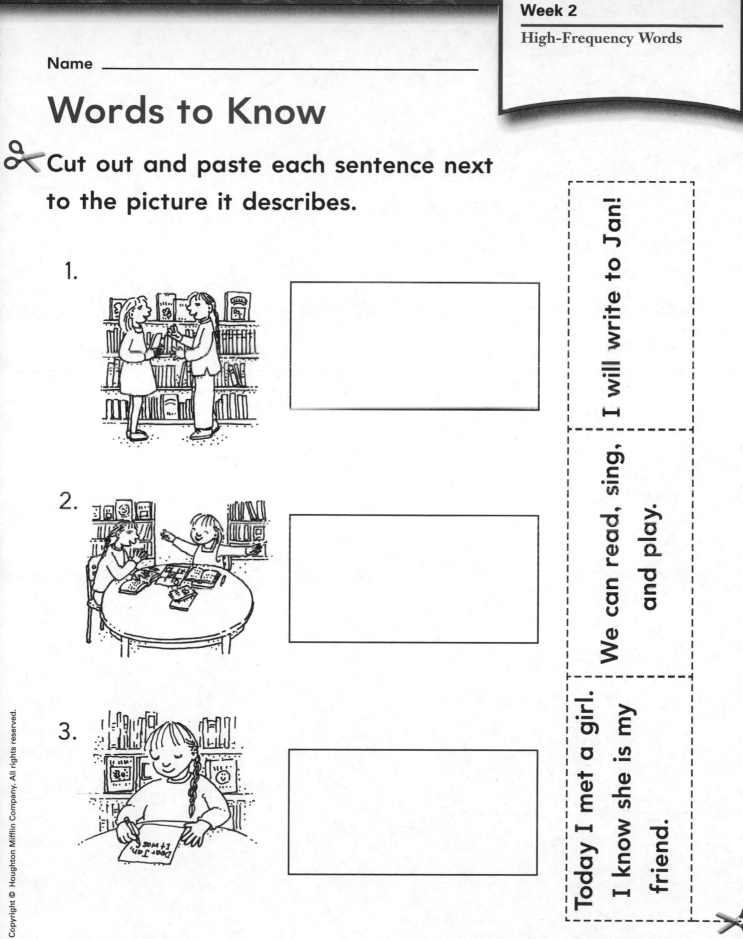

I will write to Jan!

We can read, sing, and play.

Today I met a girl. I know she is my friend.

Name ____________________

# Words to Know

Write words from the box to complete the story.

**Word Bank**

sing read today play

Fran is my best friend.

She can ____________ like a bird.

She can ____________ tricks, too.

I will write to Fran ____________ .
I will tell my best friend what I did.
I know Fran will write back.

I can ____________ what she did, too!

**Week 2**

**Story Vocabulary** *The Best Pet*

Name ______________________________

# The Big Day!

**Read the story. Draw a picture to go with it.**

One day there is a sign at the door.

Jack got a picture of a boy and his dog.

Jack got first prize, and everyone smiled.

Name ______________________

# The Best Pet Trick

Write a word from the box to complete each answer.

**Word Bank**

prize Test Peg

1. What is on the sign?
   All pets can come to the Best Pet ____________.

2. What trick did Slim do?
   Slim and ____________ did a "Knock, Knock" trick.

3. Who did the best pet trick?
   Slim did! Slim got the ____________.

Name ____________________

# The Short *e* Sound

Say each picture name. Write the word from the box that begins with the same sound.

**Spelling Words**

| | | | | | |
|---|---|---|---|---|---|
| get | ten | red | pet | men | yes |

1. 

2. 

3. 

4. 

5. 

6. 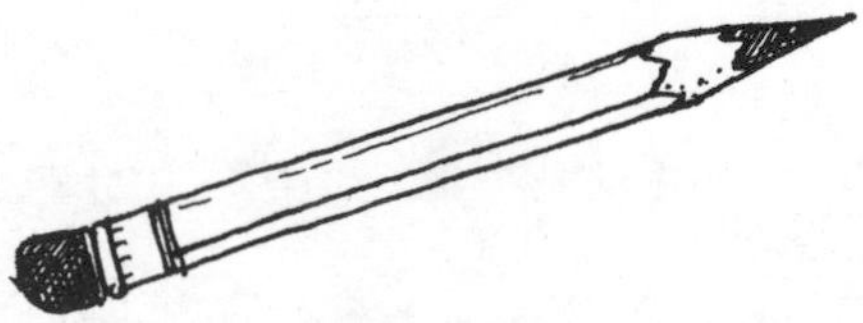

Name ______________________________

# Find the Sentence

Read each group of words. Underline each telling sentence.

Mom calls to me.

Mom

Bob sings.

sings

Dad looks at the paper.

looks at the paper

wins the prize

Bob wins the prize.

Name ______________________

# Spelling Spree

**Write the Spelling Words that rhyme with pen under the  . Write the Spelling Words that rhyme with jet under the  .**

**Spelling Words**

| | | | | | |
|---|---|---|---|---|---|
| get | ten | red | pet | men | yes |

**pen**

______________

1. ______________

3. ______________

**jet**

______________

2. ______________

4. ______________

**Proofread each sentence. Circle each Spelling Word that is wrong, and write it correctly.**

5. I like the color redd. ______________

6. Yez, I do. ______________

Name ______________________________

# Write About It!

Choose a topic. Then write some sentences about it.

**Topic:**

**Sentences:**

Name ______________________

# Triple Clusters

**Read the story. Write each word in dark print next to the picture it names.**

Big Gus **splits** the logs.
The **scraps** go in the bin.
Big Gus **scrubs** up.
He **strums** and hums.

1.  ______________________

2.  ______________________

3.  ______________________

4.  ______________________

Name ______________________

# Words with Short *u*

Write u to complete each word. Then write two of the words to complete the sentence.

1. b___s
2. dr___m
3. f___n
4. t___b
5. d___ck
6. j___st

7. The ______________ swims in the ______________ .

Name ________________________________

# Words with Short *u*

Read each word in dark print. Circle and write the rhyming word in the box.

| | | | |
|---|---|---|---|
| **bug** ________ | tug<br>sun<br>cub | **fun** ________ | but<br>luck<br>run |
| **nut** ________ | hum<br>cut<br>duck | **buzz** ________ | slug<br>rug<br>fuzz |
| **gum** ________ | club<br>plum<br>puff | **dust** ________ | must<br>hug<br>jump |

Name ______________________________

# Put Them in Order!

**Think about The Best Pet. Cut out the pictures and sentences, and paste them in order.**

| 1 | 2 | 3 |
| --- | --- | --- |
| | | |

Slim gets first prize!

The Best
Pet Test!
All pets
can come!

The girls see a sign.

Slim does a fun trick.

Name ______________________

# Words to Know

Write words from the box to complete the story.

**Word Bank**

Would walk hold hear hurt

1. My dog is ______________.

2. We ______________ the vet can help us learn why.

3. I have to ______________ my dog in the car.

4. At the vet's, we ______________ down the steps.

5. ______________ the vet help my dog?

Name ______________________________

# Words to Know

Read the story. Draw a picture to go with it.

My funny cat can learn to walk.
She falls down, but she does
not get hurt.
I do not hear Mom and Dad.
My cat hears their steps.
When we go in the car, I hold my cat.
Would you like to see my cat?

Name ______________________

# At the Pet Shop

Circle the word that completes each sentence.
Write the word.

1. Judd felt glad his big ____________ had come!

   day   down

2. He and Dad walked to the pet ____________.

   step   shop

3. "The ____________ are we get one pup," said Dad.

   read   rules

4. "I hear a ____________," said Judd. "What a pup!"

   noise   nose

Name ______________________________

# What's Happening?

Read each sentence, and look at the pictures. Circle and color the picture that shows what happens in **Bud's Day Out**.

1. Bud is Ben's pet.

2. Ben and Mom look here for Bud.

3. Ben and Mom find Bud here.

Write what happens at the end of the story.

______________________________

______________________________

Name ______________________________

# The Short u Sound

Read each clue. Write the correct Spelling Word from the box.

**Spelling Words**

| | | | | | |
|---|---|---|---|---|---|
| up | us | but | fun | cut | run |

1. not walk: ____________

2. not down: ____________

3. like we: ____________

4. what tricks are: ____________

Write the two words that rhyme with **hut**.

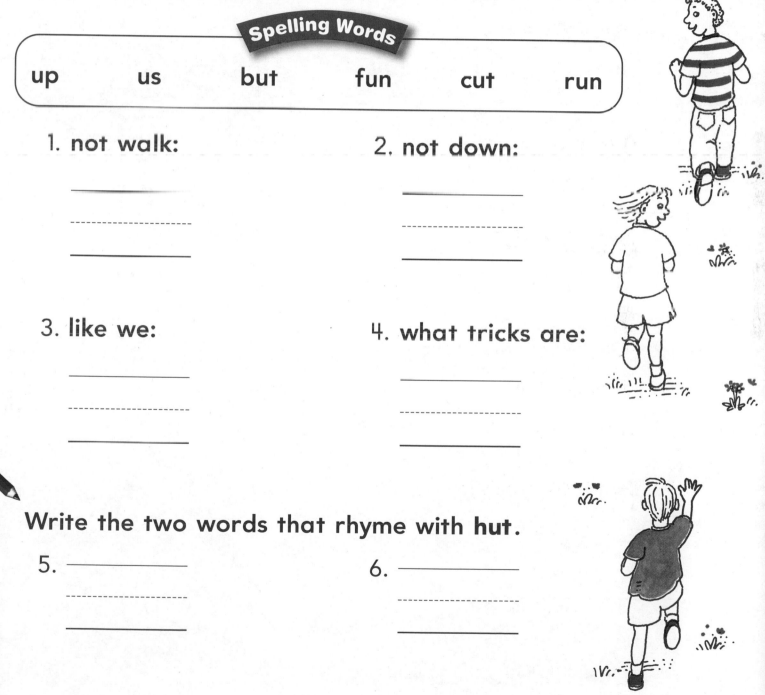

5. ____________

6. ____________

Name ______________________________

# Where's the Question?

Read each sentence. Underline each asking sentence.

1. The class play is today.

   What day is it?

2. Who is in the play?

   The play has animals.

3. Can we go to the play?

   I can write a play.

4. The play is fun.

   Where is the next play?

Name ______________________

# Spelling Spree

Use the letter shapes to make Spelling Words.

**Spelling Words**

up us but fun cut run

1. 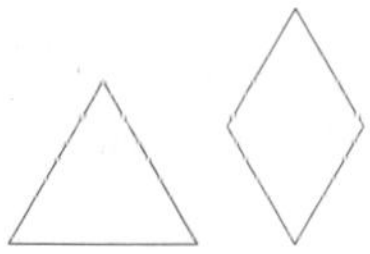
______

2. 
______

3. 
______

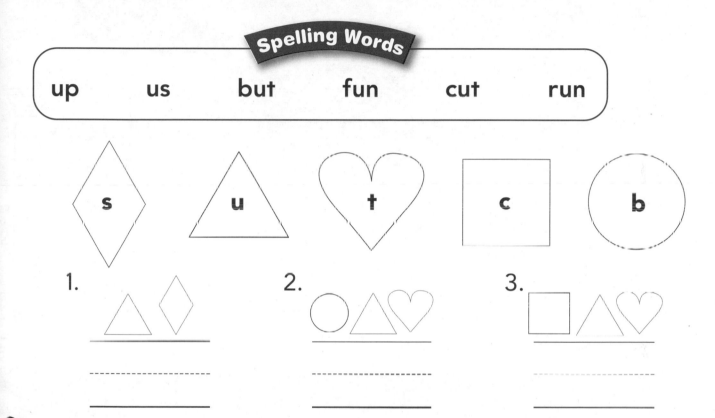

Proofread each sentence. Circle each Spelling Word that is wrong, and write it correctly.

4. I like to runn. ______

5. It is a lot of fon. ______

6. I can run ub a hill. ______

Name ______

# What's Your Question?

Write questions for each question word.

1. Who ______

2. What ______

3. Where ______

4. Why ______

Name ______________________________

# Spelling Review

Write a Spelling Word next to each number.

**Spelling Words**

on   yes   box   ten   but   fun

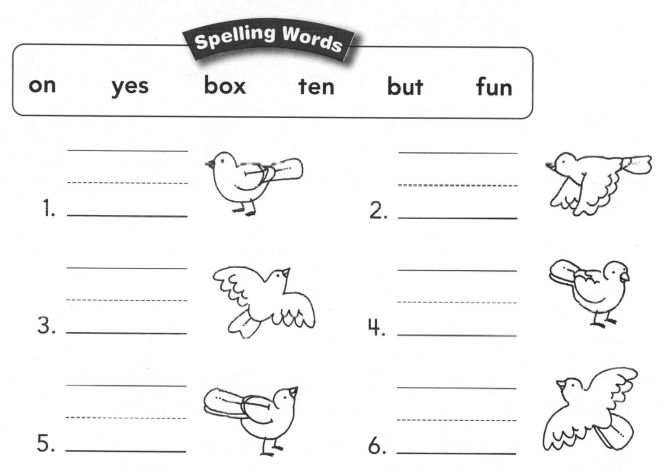

1. ______________

2. ______________

3. ______________

4. ______________

5. ______________

6. ______________

Which words have the short e sound?
Color those birds red.
Which words have the short u sound?
Color those birds blue.
Which words have the short o sound?
Color those birds brown.

Name ____________________

# Spelling Spree

Write the Spelling Word for each clue.

**Spelling Words**

hot get run yes up fun

1. not cold ____________
2. not no ____________
3. not down ____________

Proofread each sentence. Circle each Spelling Word that is wrong, and write it correctly.

4. We had fon today. ____________
5. She loves to runn and play. ____________
6. Come git your pup today! ____________

# My Handbook

# Contents

Alphafriends 194

Phonics/Decoding Strategy 196

Reading Strategies 197

Writing the Alphabet 198

Spelling
- How to Study a Word 206
- Special Words for Writing 207
- Take-Home Word Lists 209

Andy Apple

Benny Bear

Callie Cat

Dudley Duck

Edna Elephant

Fifi Fish

Gertie Goose

Hattie Horse

Iggy Iguana

Jumping Jill

Keely Kangaroo

Larry Lion

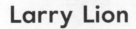

Mimi Mouse

Nyle Noodle

Ozzie Octopus

Pippa Pig

Queenie Queen

Reggie Rooster

Sammy Seal

Tiggy Tiger

Umbie Umbrella

Vinny Volcano

Willy Worm

Mr. X-Ray

Yetta Yo-Yo

Zelda Zebra

## Phonics/Decoding Strategy

1. Look at the letters from left to right.
2. Think about the sounds for the letters, and look for word parts you know.
3. Blend the sounds to read the word.
4. Ask yourself: Is it a word I know? Does it make sense in what I am reading?
5. If not, ask yourself: What else can I try?

**Predict/Infer**

- Think about the title, the illustrations, and what you have read so far.
- Tell what you think will happen next or what you will learn.

**Question**

- Ask yourself questions as you read.

**Monitor/Clarify**

- Ask yourself if what you are reading makes sense.
- If you don't understand something, reread, read ahead, or use the illustrations.

**Summarize**

- Think about the main ideas or the important parts of the story.
- Tell the important things in your own words.

**Evaluate**

- Ask yourself: Do I like what I have read? Am I learning what I wanted to know?

## Writing the Alphabet

Trace and write the letters.

Aa Aa

Bb Bb

Cc Cc

Dd Dd

Ee Ee

Ff Ff

Gg Gg

Trace and write the letters.

Hh Hh

Ii Ii

Jj Jj

Kk Kk

Ll Ll

Mm Mm

Trace and write the letters.

Nn Nn

Oo Oo

Pp Pp

Qq Qq

Rr Rr

Ss Ss

Tt Tt

Trace and write the letters.

Uu Uu

Vv Vv

Ww Ww

Xx Xx

Yy Yy

Zz Zz

Trace and write the letters.

Aa Aa

Bb Bb

Cc Cc

Dd Dd

Ee Ee

Ff Ff

Gg Gg

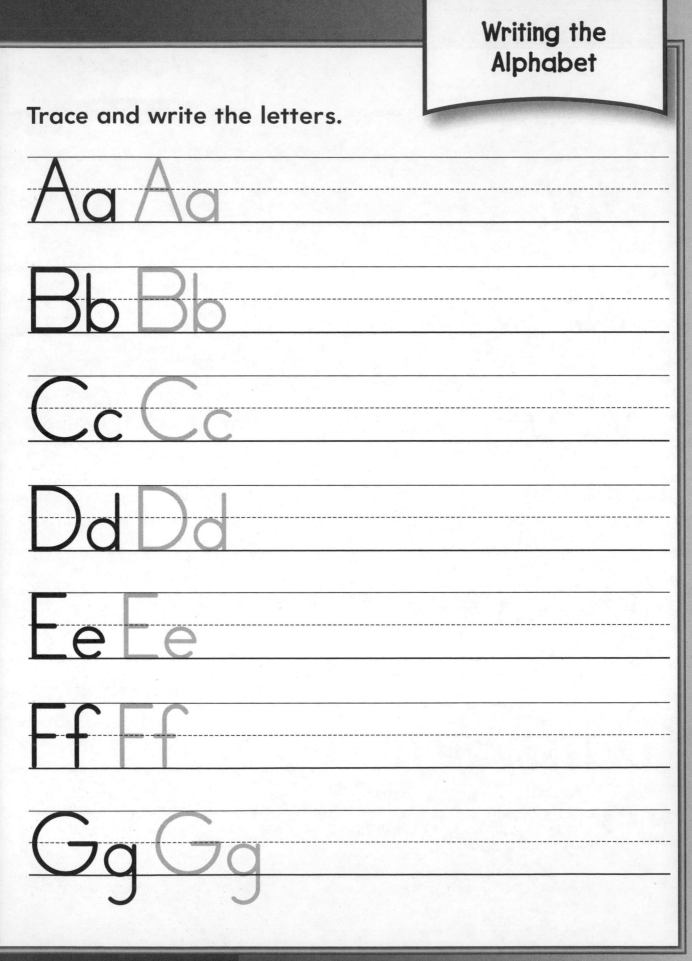

Trace and write the letters.

Hh Hh

Ii Ii

Jj Jj

Kk Kk

Ll Ll

Mm Mm

Trace and write the letters.

Nn Nn

Oo Oo

Pp Pp

Qq Qq

Rr Rr

Ss Ss

Tt Tt

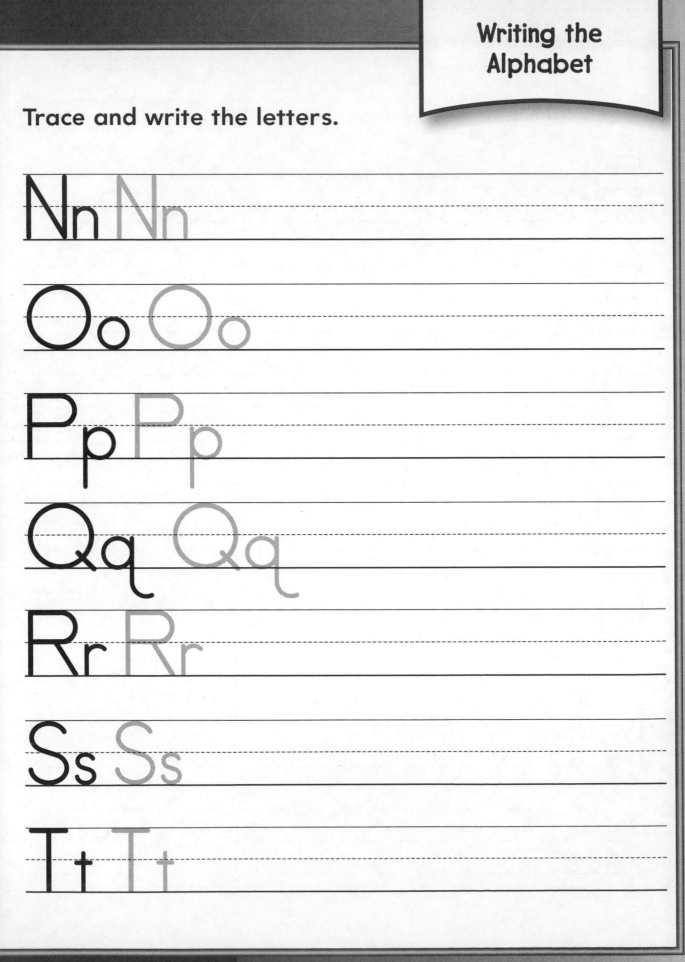

Trace and write the letters.

Uu Uu

Vv Vv

Ww Ww

Xx Xx

Yy Yy

Zz Zz

# How to Study a Word

1. LOOK at the word.
2. SAY the word.
3. THINK about the word.
4. WRITE the word.
5. CHECK the spelling.

# Special Words for Writing

**A**
a
about
again
always
and
any
around
as

**B**
back
because
before

**C**
cannot
come
coming
could

**D**
do
down

**F**
for
friend
from

**G**
getting
goes
going

**H**
has
have
her
here
his
house
how

**I**
I
if
into
is

**L**
little

**M**
many
more

**N**
never
new
now

## Special Words for Writing

**O**

of
one
or
other
our
out
over

**P**

people

**R**

right

**S**

said
some

**T**

than
the
their
there
they
thing
to
tried
two

**V**

very

**W**

want
was
were
what
when
where
who
would

**Y**

you
your

## Take-Home Word List

### Mr. C's Dinner

**The Short i sound**
in
it
him

### Spelling Words

1. in
2. it
3. him
4. big
5. sit
6. did

### Challenge Words

1. dish
2. milk

**My Study List**
Add your own spelling words on the back. →



## Take-Home Word List

### Seasons

**The Short a sound**
an
at
can

### Spelling Words

1. an
2. at
3. can
4. cat
5. had
6. man

### Challenge Words

1. catch
2. add

**My Study List**
Add your own spelling words on the back. →

## Take-Home Word List

Name

### My Study List

1.

2.

3.

4.

5.

6.



## Take-Home Word List

Name

### My Study List

1.

2.

3.

4.

5.

6.

## Take-Home Word List

### Let's Look Around!
### Spelling Review

**Spelling Words**

1. an
2. in
3. trap
4. at
5. it
6. crab
7. had
8. big
9. drip
10. grab

See the back for Challenge Words.

**My Study List**
Add your own spelling words on the back.



## Take-Home Word List

### What a Trip!

| Consonant Clusters with r | |
|---|---|
| trip | crab |
| drip | grin |

**Spelling Words**

1. trip
2. crab
3. drip
4. grin
5. grab
6. trap

**Challenge Words**

1. crack
2. brown

**My Study List**
Add your own spelling words on the back.

## Take-Home Word List

Name ____________________

### My Study List

1. ____________________
2. ____________________
3. ____________________
4. ____________________
5. ____________________
6. ____________________



## Take-Home Word List

Name ____________________

### My Study List

1. ____________________
2. ____________________
3. ____________________
4. ____________________
5. ____________________
6. ____________________

### Challenge Words

1. **add**
2. **dish**
3. **crack**

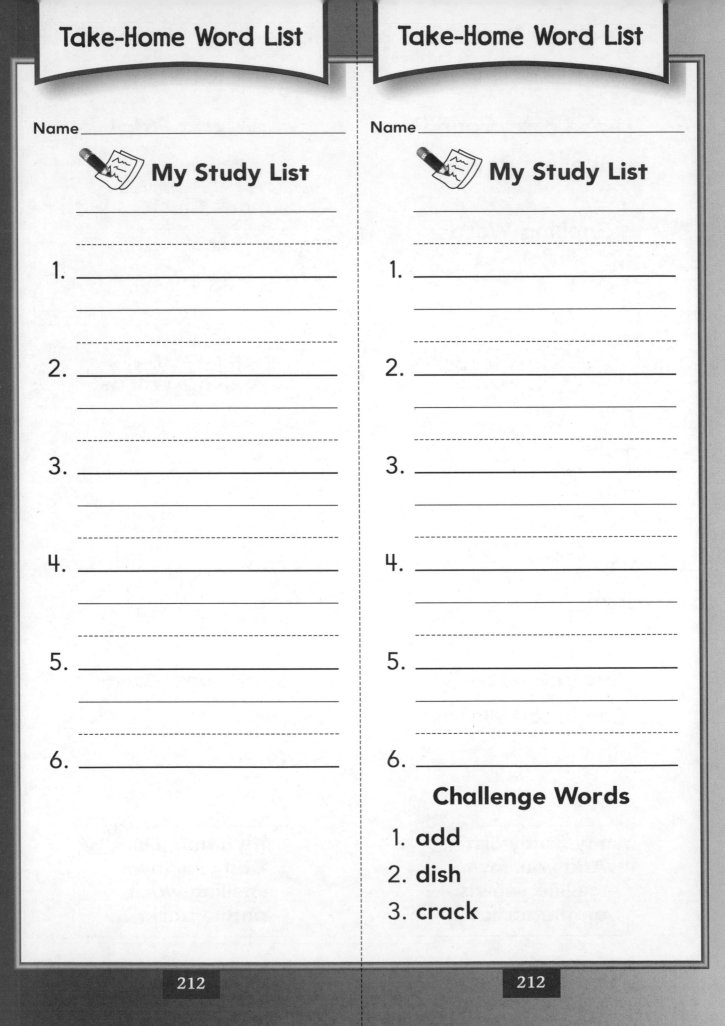

Take-Home Word List

## The Best Pet

**The Short e sound**
**get**
**ten**
**red**

### Spelling Words

1. get
2. ten
3. red
4. pet
5. men
6. yes

### Challenge Words

1. tent
2. bell

**My Study List**
Add your own spelling words on the back.





Take-Home Word List

## Who's in a Family?

**The Short o sound**
**on**
**not**
**box**

### Spelling Words

1. on
2. not
3. got
4. box
5. hot
6. top

### Challenge Words

1. pond
2. doll

**My Study List**
Add your own spelling words on the back.

## Take-Home Word List

Name ______________________

### My Study List

______________________

1. ______________________

2. ______________________

3. ______________________

4. ______________________

5. ______________________

6. ______________________



## Take-Home Word List

Name ______________________

### My Study List

______________________

1. ______________________

2. ______________________

3. ______________________

4. ______________________

5. ______________________

6. ______________________

214

## Take-Home Word List

### Family and Friends
### Spelling Review

**Spelling Words**

1. on
2. get
3. up
4. hot
5. ten
6. but
7. box
8. fun
9. yes
10. run

**See the back for Challenge Words.**

**My Study List**
Add your own spelling words on the back.



## Take-Home Word List

### Bud's Day Out

**The Short u sound**
up
us
but

**Spelling Words**

1. up
2. us
3. but
4. fun
5. cut
6. run

**Challenge Words**

1. jump
2. plum

**My Study List**
Add your own spelling words on the back.

## Take-Home Word List

Name ______________________

### My Study List

1. ______________________
2. ______________________
3. ______________________
4. ______________________
5. ______________________
6. ______________________



## Take-Home Word List

Name ______________________

### My Study List

1. ______________________
2. ______________________
3. ______________________
4. ______________________
5. ______________________
6. ______________________

### Challenge Words

1. pond
2. bell
3. plum

216

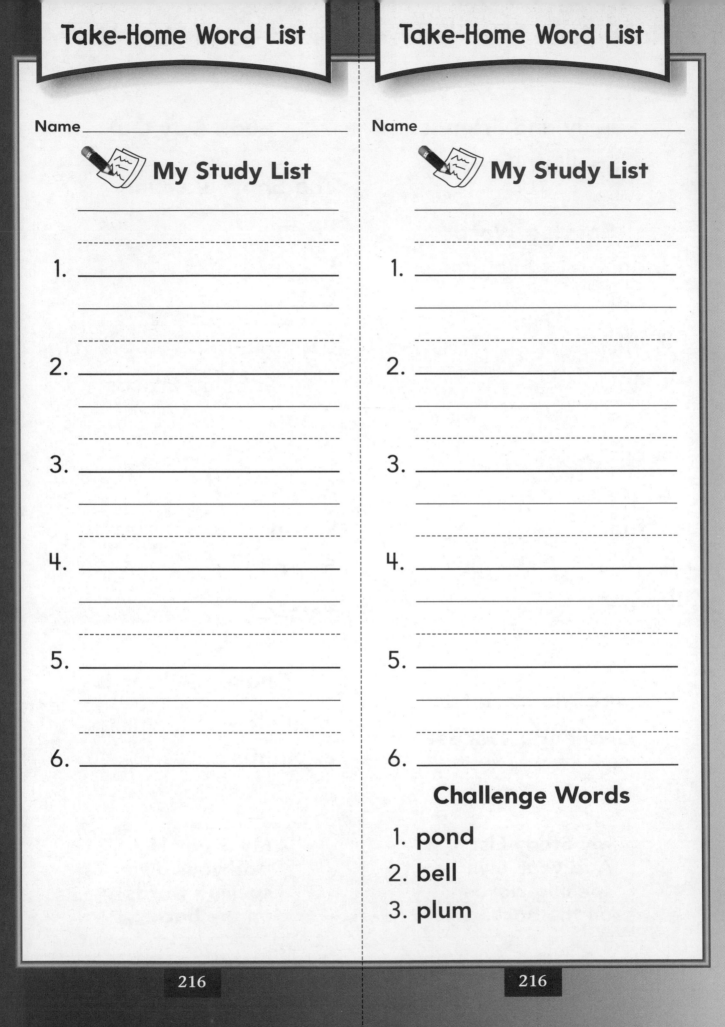

| | | | | | | | | |
|---|---|---|---|---|---|---|---|---|
| A | A | A | B | B | C | C | D | D |
| E | E | E | F | F | G | G | H | H |
| I | I | J | J | K | K | L | L | M |
| M | N | N | O | O | P | P | Q | Q |
| R | R | S | S | T | T | U | U | V |
| V | W | W | X | X | Y | Y | Z | Z |

You can add punctuation marks or other letters to the blanks.

**Letter Tray**

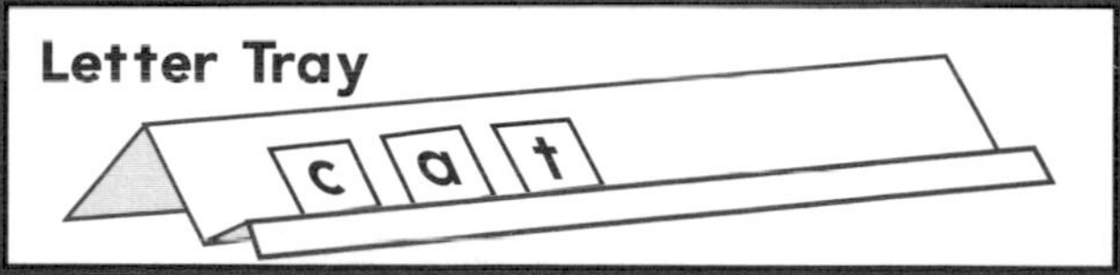


fold

fold

fold

| | | | | | | | | |
|---|---|---|---|---|---|---|---|---|
| d | d | c | c | b | b | a | a | a |
| h | h | g | g | f | f | e | e | e |
| m | l | l | k | k | j | j | i | i |
| q | q | p | p | o | o | n | n | m |
| v | u | u | t | t | s | s | r | r |
| z | z | y | y | x | x | w | w | v |

fold

fold

fold

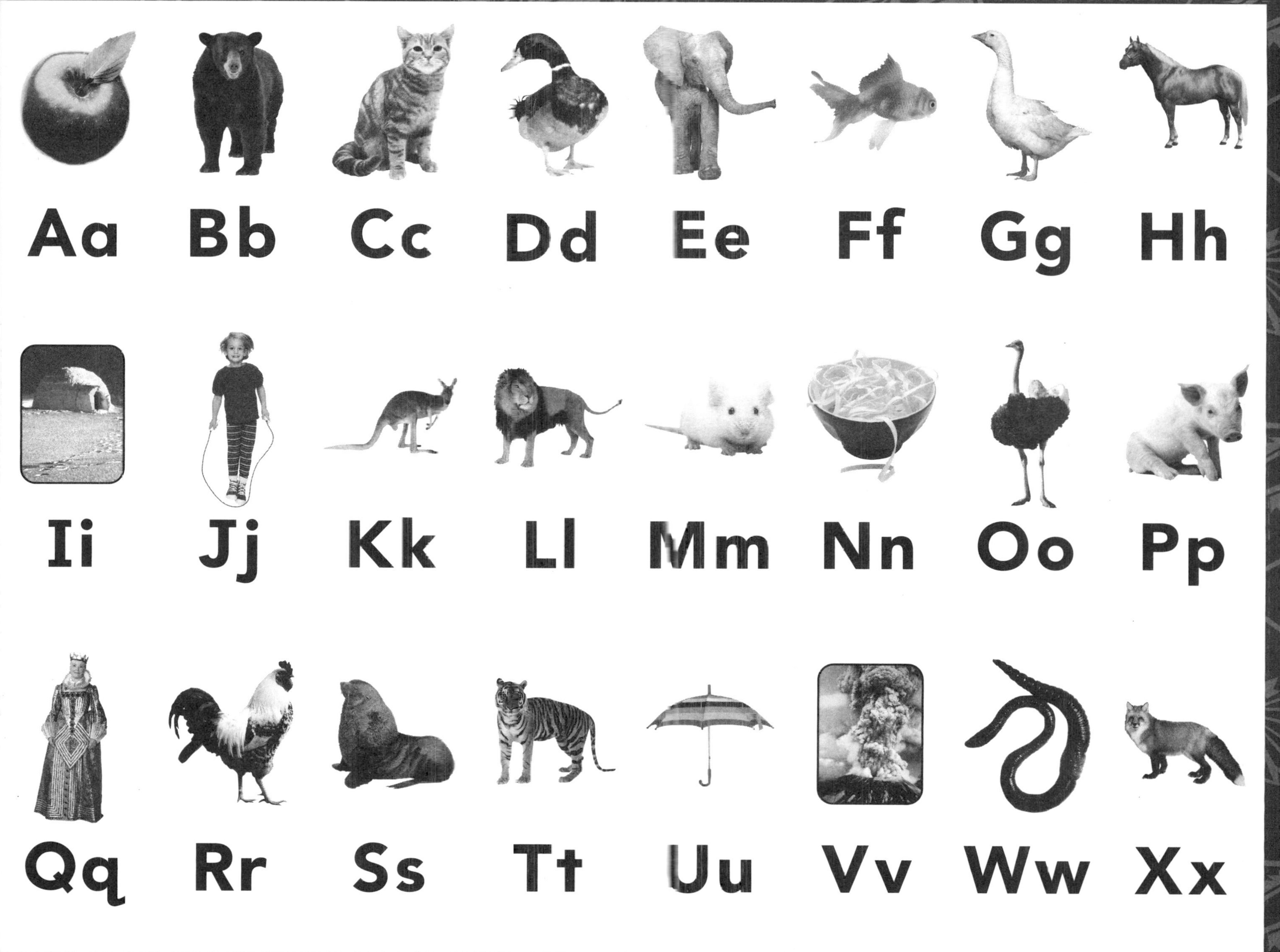

Aa Bb Cc Dd Ee Ff Gg Hh
Ii Jj Kk Ll Mm Nn Oo Pp
Qq Rr Ss Tt Uu Vv Ww Xx

a

b

c
k
_ck

d
_ed

e

f

g

h

i

j
ge
gi_
_dge

k
c
_ck

l
_le

m

n
kn_
gn

o

p

qu_

r
wr_

s
ce
ci_

t
_ed

u

v

w

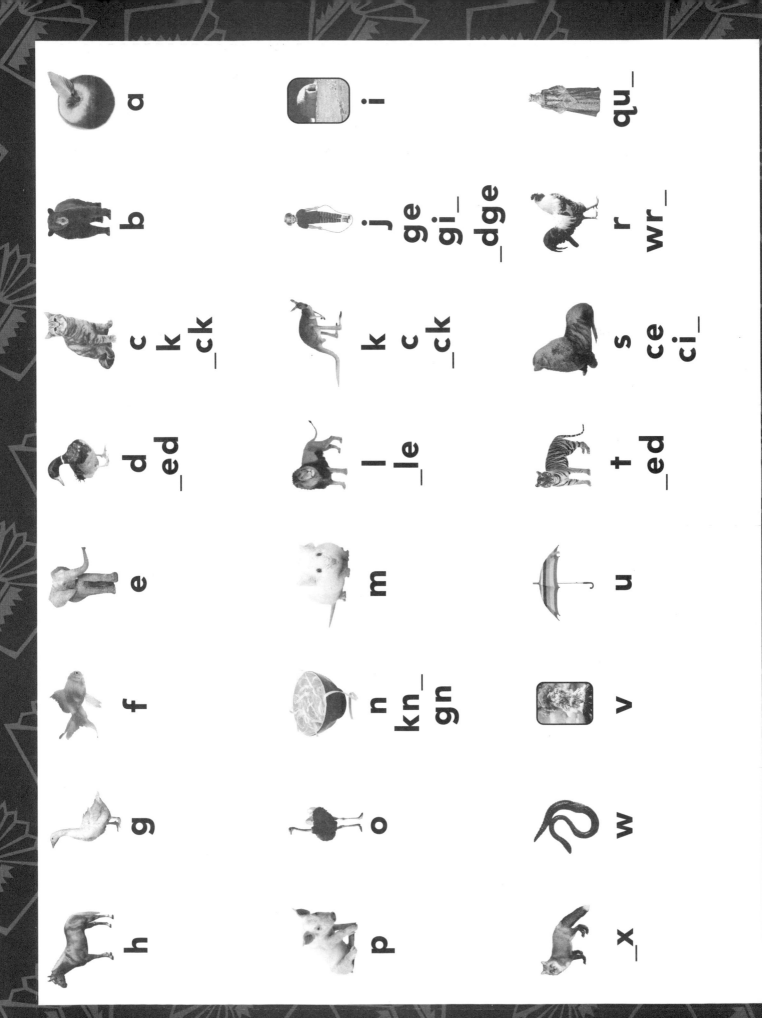

_x

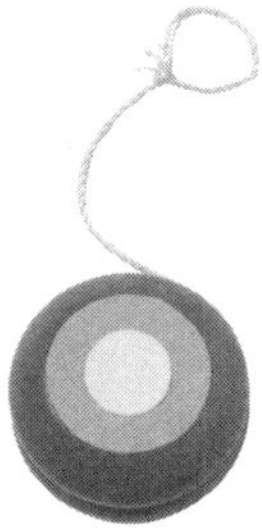
Yy

Zz

sh
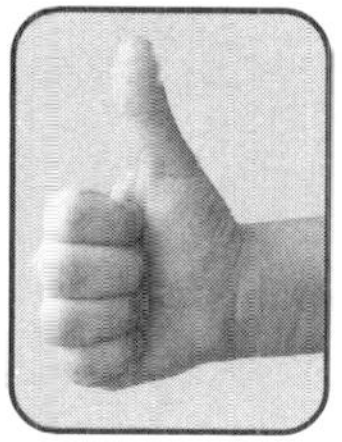
th

wh

ch

a

i

o

u

e

oo
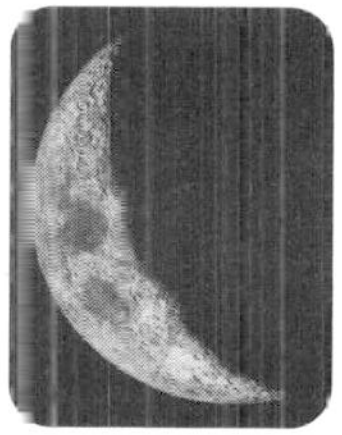
oo

ow

oy

aw

or

ir

ar

i
i_e
ie
igh
_y

a
a_e
ai
_ay

ch
_tch

wh

th

sh

z
_s

y_

aw
au

_oy
oi

ow
ou

oo
ew
ue
ou
u
u_e

oo

e
e_e
ee
ea
_y
_ie_

u
u_e
_ue
ew

o
o_e
oa
ow
_oe

ar

ir
er
ur

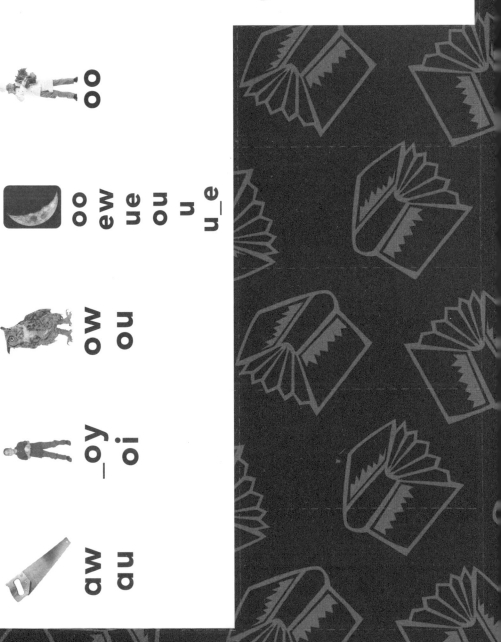

or
ore

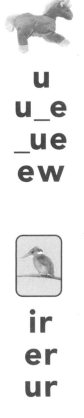

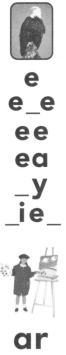

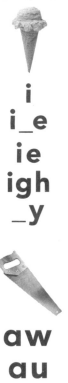